Testimonials

"*Do you sometimes feel helpless and lost or maybe even taken advantage of when it comes to all things financial in your life?* In MONEY TRUTH & LIFE, Judy debunks financial myths and lends eye-opening truth in a very practical way. You will easily be able to apply her message to your personal life and find true freedom and turn around. *Judy is a woman of great wisdom and sincerely practices what she preaches.* Her passion to share her knowledge and understanding in a down-to-earth and clear way for *every* individual to understand is made plain in this script. *We have seen and experienced firsthand the fruit of what she speaks about in her life and family* and it is a joy to witness her authentic strength in action!"

> **Matt & Tabea Oppliger,** Founders
> and Directors of KitePride,
> a social business in Tel Aviv, Israel

"Learning and activating the five pillars of finance that Judy shares in this book will positively impact your finances and take your life to a new level."

> **Dr. Bob Harrison,** "*America's Increase Authority*"

"In personal and business advice, I love the value of robust simplicity. In other words, that which is fundamentally simple and invariably reliable. MONEY TRUTH & LIFE is a simple primer on the truth about money and a fulfilled financial life. Don't miss the value of this book because of its simplicity; therein lies its profound value."

"Judy Copenbarger's credibility comes from an authentic desire to truly help people and from her abundant generosity. She has a background of formal legal training and is an amazingly intelligent and energetic learner and teacher. Use this book to check your own financial wisdom and pass it on as a trusted resource to someone you love."

Jeff Abbott, Convene Business Coach and Mentor

"Today people are challenged by money, and this book helps you build a *solid* financial future."

Stephen Christensen, Chief Development Officer, Olive Crest—transforming lives of at-risk children; Former Dean, School of Business, Concordia University; Founder, Teen Entrepreneur Academy and Kid Entrepreneur Academy

"If you're looking for a way to make sense of your finances, this is the book for you! Judy pulls from her years of experience in family financial planning to break down myths and explain

difficult to understand concepts in a clear and engaging way. Using examples and stories, Judy helps us all wisely navigate the potential pitfalls and obstacles that cause so many of us to stumble. MONEY TRUTH & LIFE is an essential guide that will help you experience financial freedom and peace in a whole new way!"

Michael Mistretta, CEO of FIRM:
Fellowship of Israel Related Ministries

"MONEY TRUTH & LIFE provides a concise and thorough overview for handling your finances, whether you are young and just getting started or older and looking at retirement. Judy Copenbarger's definitions and advice are eye-opening and helpfully clear for dealing with personal, family, or business financial needs. This book makes a perfect wedding present or graduation present. I'll order several!! I'm going to give it to every graduate!"

Elizabeth L. Glanville, MA, MA, PhD
Fuller Seminary—Professor,
Doctor of Intercultural Studies/
Doctor of Missiology program on leadership

"I have known Judy Copenbarger for well over 15 years both professionally and socially with her husband Larry. Her passion is deep-rooted for helping families understand Biblical financial principles and most importantly applying them. Her new book,

MONEY TRUTH & LIFE sums up that passion for you. Judy has a remarkable way of taking complex concepts and presenting them in a very practical way. Since work and finances tend to go hand in hand, being a good steward of the skills and abilities that God has entrusted to each of us will reap rewards in heaven. MONEY TRUTH & LIFE is a great study guide for your journey to be that good steward!"

Jim Sullivan, CEO,
Co-Founder of Vision Resourcing Group

"This book is like a textbook for your financial life. There is so much *valuable* information contained in these pages that you should refer to it when you make any financial decisions. When you're being told something you're not familiar with, *this book could save you a lot of pain.* Read, read, and read again and then keep it near you as a ready resource for moving forward!"

Pastor Brent Bailey, B.S. Th.D.
Direction Church Orlando,
FL & Host of the Cabin Fever Podcast

"MONEY TRUTH & LIFE *will make all the difference in your life.* If you are ready to understand your finances, once and for all, please study this book. It will be the best thing you've ever done. *My wife and I have trusted Judy with every major financial decision*

for decades and we are all the better for it. She has helped us with our legacy planning, taxes, retirement planning, and beyond. Her compassionate and attentive nature, along with her patience, has given us comfort and confidence to retire well beyond our expectations. These principles really work!"

Dr. J. Robert Clinton, Fuller Seminary,
Director, School of Intercultural Studies,
professor of leadership, renowned author

"Remarkably practical and easy to put into action, the advice that Judy dispenses is honest, reassuring, and humane. I personally was excited about the extension of her knowledge offered in her Mastery Program, designed to walk us through financial success. I wholeheartedly recommend MONEY TRUTH & LIFE!"

"I have known Judy for years now and I can tell you that her wisdom and positive attitude come shining through in this book. No matter your level of financial understanding, you will learn something new in these pages. If you feel shackled by financial burden, the truths in this book will likely set you free to experience true living. I'm more prepared to handle my finances because I read MONEY TRUTH & LIFE"

Tom Munson, Chairman,
C12: National CEO Leadership Roundtables

MONEY
TRUTH
&LIFE

MONEY TRUTH
& LIFE

PRACTICAL WISDOM TO
STRENGTHEN FAMILIES FOR LIFE

BY JUDY L. COPENBARGER, JD, CFP®, AIF®

Published by
Impact Driven Publishing
3129 S. Hacienda Boulevard, Suite #658
Hacienda Heights, CA 91745

Manufactured in the United States of America, or in the United Kingdom when distributed elsewhere.

Copenbarger, Judy
MONEY TRUTH & LIFE: Practical Wisdom to Strengthen Families for Life
LCCN: 2020905703
ISBN: 978-1-7347528-2-3
eBook: 978-1-7347528-3-0

Cover design and Logo by: Bob Payne
Author photo by: Donna Edman Photography
Illustrations by: Bob Payne / Vera Milosavich
Copyediting by: Elizabeth Ann Marks / Lara Kennedy
Interior design by: Medlar Publishing Solutions Pvt Ltd., India

www.JudyCopenbarger.com

This book is dedicated to everyone young and old,
educated and uneducated,
employed and unemployed,
who aspires to become financially independent
and build a rewarding, happy and sustainably
successful life.
You inspire me.

Special Thanks to

My husband, Larry,
   for inspiring me to grow, share and thrive.

Our children, Brenna, Lindsay, Nicholas, Evan and Laurel
(listed youngest to eldest for a change)
   for honoring me by how they live their lives and in every other way
   possible.

My parents, Olon and Eva,
   for leading me by example, wisdom and dedication; then and now.

Our clients,
   for trusting me with their passion, purpose, dreams, goals, and
   financial decisions.

Our team,
   for supporting me with their guidance and expertise.

Barbara Bennett	Copenbarger Corp.	Manuscript Editing
Lindsay Richter	Copenbarger Corp.	Concept and Integration
Rich Kozak	RichBrands	Brand Congruence, Publication, Project Lead
	Impact Driven Publishing	Publisher
Elizabeth Ann Marks	SmartCopyClicks	Concept and Draft Editing
Bob Payne	BlueZStudios	Logo, Cover Design, Illustrations
Vera Milosavich	Vera Milosavich Illustration	Illustrations
Donna Edman	Donna Edman Photography	Brand Photography
Karen Strauss	Hybrid Global Publishing	Sr. Publisher
Sara Foley	Hybrid Global Publishing	Publishing Project Coordinator
Lara Kennedy		Copy Editing
Sundar Maruthu	Medlar Publishing Solutions	Typesetting

CONTENTS

CHAPTER 1
THE TRUTH ABOUT MONEY

How do I know when I have enough?

Why is it so hard to make ends meet?

Could I be better protecting myself financially?

When and how should I give my family something?

We have so many questions about money. And there are always new ones. So how do we find the answers? How do we sift through all the answers out there to find the answers that are right for us? That's the real question.

How can we know what's right for us?

WHERE SHOULD I PUT MY DOLLAR?

For decades, clients have been walking in through the doors of my offices asking the same question over and over. They ask this question in many ways. They ask this question in many contexts and seasons of life. Here's the question:

"I have a dollar. What should I do with it?" Of course, you have several dollars (and other measurements of currency) to allocate, so where do you start?

You have dollars set aside for daily and monthly personal expenses and perhaps business expenses. You have dollars that are used to protect what you have accumulated, such as insurance premiums and legal protections. You have dollars that are allocated to growth for future goals and endeavors. Some of your money is intended for gifting to your family and favorite causes, both now and in the future.

MONEY IS A VALUABLE TOOL

Your money is a valuable tool to be used for everything from the necessities of food, shelter, clothing, transportation, and family care to the activities, endeavors, and adventures that make your life special. Beyond the fundamental expenses in life, you may choose to help other people and causes that you care about and find fulfillment in the way you choose to allocate your dollars.

GETTING IT RIGHT

Most of us did not enjoy a formal financial education. Many of us learned about money through trial and error, asking other people, researching on the internet, or perusing popular financial books. Perhaps you had the advantage of a parent or mentor who taught you how to best earn, spend, save, manage, give, and protect your dollars. Perhaps you received an education that bestowed on you knowledge and information to help you manage your dollars well. Maybe you have made enough money mistakes that you now know what works and what doesn't work so well.

Your burning question may simply be about how to get the money thing right. It is not easy.

You are a Target

An important principle to consider is that the financial industry, in general, is not about you at all. You are a means to an end for most financial companies, banks, wire houses, brokers, dealers, and financial consultants. You are the target for many sales organizations that appear to be in a service industry. There are usually incentives, enticements, commissions, and transactions involved with any financial advice you receive out in the world.

Your "advice" may come from a television personality, self-acclaimed expert, professionally dressed agent in an office or bank, author, or well-meaning relative. It is always advisable to consider the source. Why would this person give me this recommendation? Is it the best course of action for me? What is the downside to this action if I fully implement it? What will my true cost of time and money be? Is there an easier or more efficient way to get the same or a better result?

In some circumstances, a "do it yourself" approach may cause less damage and risk than implementing costly advice. The inherent risk to doing it yourself is that you may miss important activities, duplicate your actions, incur unnecessary expenses, and waste time. You don't know what you don't know. To learn more about efficiently planning for your financial future, check out www.JudyCopenbarger. com/truth.

GROW AND PROTECT

As you reflect on your personal financial journey, what you've learned, and what you would like to master next, you may find that experience has been your best teacher to date. Consider what caused you to engage with this information. What would you like to know? How could a fresh perspective help you as you move forward in your life?

You are about to explore the fundamentals of money, ways to apply financial principles in your life, and the actions and outcomes you can expect with having learned these things. Even slight modifications in your priorities and perspectives will change the trajectory of your financial success, future, and freedom. Please congratulate yourself for embarking on this journey. Most people never do this. Most people never get this right.

CHAPTER 2

FUNDAMENTALS OF MONEY

Strategic Financial Planning can be overwhelming. It may help for you to break down the five fundamental pillars of finance (money) and approach them one at a time.

You will find that every decision that you make about your money is rooted in at least one of the five fundamental pillars of finance. Every choice you make about your finances is determined by your attitude, discipline, and habits in these five areas.

The five pillars of finance are Taxation, Legal, Cashflow Planning, Asset Management, and Insurances.

Taxation, Legal, and Insurances are primarily the Protection elements of your strategic financial planning. Consider these aspects to be the defensive plays in your ongoing game. Taxation, Legal, and Insurances strategic planning make up your Financial Greenhouse "Structure." These are your asset protection activities.

Cashflow Planning and Asset Management are primarily the Growth elements of your strategic financial planning. Consider these aspects to be the offensive plays in your ongoing game. Cashflow Planning and Asset Management make up your Financial Greenhouse "Garden." These are your asset growth activities.

CHAPTER 3

HOW TO PLAN FOR TAXATION TO ELIMINATE STRESS & ANXIETY

Taxation Planning is the fundamental pillar of finance that surprises most people.

Most people do not have formal training in tax law, tax planning, or tax return preparation, but every person is forced to participate in the taxation process annually. As a result, a significant amount of shock and awe is associated with ideals and expectations around taxes.

Your CPA is not Your Trust Attorney

Although a CPA is qualified to understand and apply current tax laws, CPAs are not necessarily planners. They may have a basic understanding of trust documents, but most are not particularly skilled in contracts or estate planning law. Here's what happened to Mabel and Ted.

Although she was perky, energetic, and healthy for many years, when her husband died, Mabel succumbed to pneumonia over the holidays just a year later.

Mabel and her husband, Ted, had created a marital trust when they were younger. They were diligent to update it throughout their marriage and were careful to title all assets in their trust's name.

When Ted passed away, Mabel visited her CPA to finalize the marital tax return and showed her CPA their marital trust. They had a disclaimer trust. Mabel didn't know what that meant, and unfortunately, neither did her CPA. She was advised that there was nothing to be done and no reason to spend the time or money to talk to her attorney.

This mistaken advice was extremely costly to Mabel and her children.

A disclaimer trust requires that within nine months of the death of the first spouse to die, a formal notice must be prepared and appropriately exercised. In Mabel's case, within months after Ted's passing, she was required to prepare this paperwork to avoid the estate tax on his half of the estate. Because her CPA advised her not to do this, her family ended up paying an additional $420,000 in estate taxes to the IRS upon her death as a result of the poor advice that she received.

Please be aware of the type of trust you have and whether disclaimer provisions apply to you. If you have a disclaimer trust, the best action you can take is to revise or replace it to exclude this limiting language. There are several good reasons not to have it and no good reasons to have it.

Caution: Bad Tax Advice is Devastating

Some CPAs are blessed with an entrepreneurial spirit, but please beware of those who are too aggressive, as in the case of Troy and Donna.

They had three different businesses between them that were doing well. Their CPA approached them with an opportunity to carry forward their net losses from one year of reorganization. It seemed to make sense. The $5,000 they paid seemed reasonable in the context of recovering $45,000 back from the IRS. They were grateful for their CPA's suggestion of an amended return and proud of themselves for their diligence.

Two years later, they received an IRS letter stating that their amended return was incorrect and they owed $45,000 plus the additional penalties and interest. The tax bill they owed had grown to $79,000. They knew this couldn't possibly be true, so they contacted their CPA to have the CPA communicate and interpret their amended return with the IRS. Their CPA informed them there was nothing they could do because a form had to have been filed with a prior return, which the CPA was unaware of and had failed to file. Troy was very upset, and Donna fell into an emotional depression for six months. Over time, they paid the $79,000 back to the IRS and continued to grow their businesses, but they never heard from the CPA again. And he never apologized.

This $79,000 mistake gave Donna and Troy a new perspective and respect for the CPAs and tax professionals that diligently put their clients' needs above their own.

To understand some of the taxes and tax rules that apply to most people, let's explore some of the taxation basics.

INCOME TAXATION

For most people in the United States, there are two income tax returns that must be filed annually. The first is for the IRS (Federal Income Taxes), and the second is for the state in which the individual is a resident. Currently, some states do not have a tax on income.

To properly calculate income taxes, important issues for the taxpayer to identify are the category of filing and sources of income.

CATEGORY OF FILING

The appropriate category of filing is determined by the IRS. The five filing status categories are: Single, Married Filing Jointly, Married Filing Separately, Head of Household, and Qualifying Widow(er) with Dependent Child.

Because there are specific advantages to filing a tax return with a certain filing status, it is important to use the expertise of your financial planner, tax attorney, or tax preparer to choose your best option. The tax rates, which are the percentages of tax to be paid, in each category vary from one another. Generally, you would choose to pay fewer tax dollars rather than more tax dollars, wouldn't you?

SOURCE OF INCOME

Considering the Source of Income is an important element to understanding how your taxes are calculated. The source of income will determine how much tax is to be paid or if there is any tax due at all. The sources include wages (Form W-2), independent contractor and unearned income (Form 1099), and trust and corporate income (Form K-1).

If you are an employee and you have a job that pays a salary or hourly wage, you receive a W-2 form annually. The W-2 form is a United States IRS tax form that each employer completes for each of their employees. This form notifies the IRS of the amount of wages earned and the amount of taxes that were withheld from the wages. Withholdings are sent to the IRS, crediting the tax account of each employee as the income is earned. This "prepaid tax" is part of the difference between the money you earn and the money you receive each pay period.

You may have income that you earn for your efforts other than wages, salaries, and tips. If you have rental property, are an independent contractor, or have income from sales, interest, or dividends, you will receive a 1099 form. The 1099 form is a United States IRS tax form that is used to notify the IRS that you have received money and that federal or state taxes may be due.

Specific 1099 forms identify the source and nature of income; for example, interest income is reported on the 1099-INT form, dividends income is reported on the 1099-DIV form, sales proceeds are reported on the 1099-B form, and miscellaneous income is reported on the 1099-MISC form.

ACTIVE INCOME VS. PASSIVE INCOME

It is important to note that some income is considered Active and some income is considered Passive for retirement planning purposes. In general, if you use your time, talent, and skill to earn the money (earned income), it will qualify for annual retirement program contributions. If your investments or real estate revenue were the source of the income (unearned income), it will not qualify for annual retirement program contributions.

CAPITAL GAINS TAXATION

Capital Gains Tax is a tax that is due in the United States when you realize a profit upon the sale of your assets. When you sell your real property, stocks, bonds, or precious metals for an amount greater than what you paid for them, your profit is taxable. For most people, the capital gains tax rates are lower than their ordinary tax rates; however, this is not always true.

There are many exceptions to this general rule. To properly calculate or estimate a capital gains tax, it is important to determine the basis of an asset (which may be more than the purchase price), the ownership and title (individual, corporate, or trust), and investment characterization (qualified or non-qualified). A substantial percentage of tax calculation mistakes are made in this area. Rely on your financial planner, tax attorney, or tax preparer to avoid a costly tax mistake.

For additional ways to keep more of what you earn, visit www.JudyCopenbarger.com/truth. Learn about our complete online money management course and how it can benefit your entire family through The **MONEY TRUTH & LIFE** *Online* **MASTERY PROGRAM.**

ESTATE AND GIFT TAXATION

Estate and Gift Taxes are both parts of an integrated tax system in the United States. Estate taxes apply to transfers of property upon a person's death, and gift taxes apply to transfers of property during a person's life.

ESTATE TAXES

When someone dies in the United States, a federal tax on the value of the Taxable Estate is due. This tax is currently as high as 40% of the gross estate value. This tax is paid by the estate of the person who died, the donor (decedent), rather than the person who is the recipient of the estate, or donee (beneficiary).

Some states also impose a State EstateTax, which adds to the percentage of tax due before beneficiaries receive their inheritance. Some states impose a State Inheritance Tax, which incurs a tax on the person receiving the money. This tax is paid by the donee rather than the donor.

Here's the good news. The Federal Estate Tax has an exemption amount. This is an amount that can be transferred to beneficiaries without applying the tax. This exemption amount is set by Congress and is frequently updated. In recent US tax history, the exemption amount has been set as low as $600,000 and as high as $11,580,000. There was even one year in which the federal estate tax was completely exempted.

Using an example of a $11,580,000 exemption, the federal estate tax would not be applied to an estate until the gross value of the estate exceeds $11,580,000 for each donor. For a married couple with proper

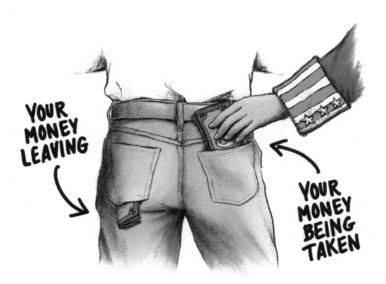

YOUR
MONEY
LEAVING

YOUR
MONEY
BEING
TAKEN

estate planning, that exemption amount would be doubled. First, to determine your federal estate tax, you would subtract $11,580,000 from your estate's gross estate value. This is your taxable estate value. No tax money is due until your estate value exceeds this current exemption amount. This is a relief for many United States citizens.

GIFT TAXES

Gift Taxes are due when someone transfers property, including cash, to another person during their life. This tax is paid by the person giving, not receiving, the money—the donor rather than the donee. You may be asking, "What? I have to pay taxes when I give something away?" The answer is … it depends, and probably not.

Current IRS rules require a gift tax return when an annual gift is given in excess of the annual Gift Exemption. This gift exemption can change in any given tax year and has been set as high as $15,000. All annual gift amounts under the gift exemption amount are exempt from reporting and from the federal gift tax. There is no limitation on the number of people to whom you can give. A married couple can join their gifts to give twice the exemption amount per year to each person with no tax due and no tax return filing requirement. With an example of a $15,000 annual gift exemption, a couple could give $30,000 to any person or people they choose. The couple is not limited to gifts of $30,000 during the year, but may give away $30,000 to more than one person or to many people.

It is also helpful to understand that a direct payment to an institution for medical bills or education is not considered to be part of the taxable gift. You could pay a hospital or university on behalf of a loved one without triggering this tax.

The good news is this: Filing a gift tax return does not mean that a tax is due and payable. Your gift tax will only be due when the accumulated gifts you make during your lifetime exceed your estate and gift tax lifetime exemption. Remember that this exemption amount has been as high as $11,580,000 each. If you strategically plan your giving, you may be able to transfer substantial assets to others without incurring a tax or ever filing a gift tax return.

Consider a conservative approach to your estate planning, because you can never know exactly what the exemption amount will be in the year of your passing.

For these gifting strategies, time is your friend. If you are inclined to give to others, consider starting as soon as possible to give as much as possible, while minimizing or mitigating the estate and gift tax impact.

FRANCHISE AND SALES TAXATION

Most of the United States have a Franchise Tax, which imposes a tax on business organizations, corporations, and partnerships for the privilege of doing business in the state. Franchise tax is based on a calculation determined by the value of the business or the capital the business holds. When determining the domicile or residence of your business (the state where it is headquartered), it is important to understand the different tax treatment of businesses in each state.

Some states are much more or much less favorable to businesses in terms of business organization tax treatment. If given a choice, you'll want to choose the state that optimizes your corporate operations, financial cashflow, and taxation circumstances.

Many municipalities (parishes, counties, cities, districts) and states have a Sales Tax. There are two parts to sales tax, namely, tax paid by the seller and tax paid by the purchaser of the goods. Business organizations, corporations, and partnerships will pay taxes calculated and based on the value of goods sold or services offered. Sales tax is also paid by the purchaser, of which you will be aware from your life experience.

Excise Taxes are imposed on purchases or activities and are usually driven by public policy. Consumption Taxes include an increase in your bottom-line cost for activities such as highway usage by trucks or taxes on gasoline at the pump. Excise taxes are calculated on a per-unit basis rather than by percentage of the fixed price. For most states, luxury taxes are due upon the purchase of nonessential items, including certain classes of jewelry, furs, cars, yachts, tobacco products, and alcohol. Thresholds of value determine whether a tax will be applicable. For example, many states will not impose this tax on a new vehicle with a value under a set amount. This value has been as high as $60,000.

An example of an excise tax that surprises some people is the tax imposed on a premature withdrawal of retirement funds. An "additional" excise tax of 10% is imposed on IRA, other employer retirement program, and 529 educational savings program distributions if the money is withdrawn at an improper time or for an improper purpose, without a specific exception. Please beware.

REAL PROPERTY TAX

The most important variables to consider in Real Property Tax are how the tax basis is calculated and how frequently it is increased. Each state has a different percentage of tax, ranging from .25% to over 2% annually. Some states reassess the value of the taxable property annually, while others reassess the property only when it is transferred to a new owner. If given a choice, you will want to choose a favorable state in which you live or own investment or business property. The tax treatment of owning real property varies greatly and is determined by location, location, location.

CHAPTER 4

How to Legally Protect
Yourself & Your Family

Legal and Legacy Planning is the fundamental pillar of finance that provides protection for family and business interests.

With so many areas of law to master, it is shocking how many self-appointed "legal experts" there are. Few have formal training, yet folks are always ready to give advice. This input could be appropriately categorized as barbershop advice or coffee shop advice.

Well-meaning relatives and colleagues are willing to share heartfelt advice and information without the benefit of knowing what they don't know.

Let's explore some fundamental estate and legacy planning principles.

PROTECTING YOUR FAMILY

We are fortunate in our country to have a court system that provides protection for individuals who cannot protect themselves. When we need the protection, we are grateful. When the court system interferes with our wishes for our older loved ones, disabled family members, or minor children, however, the impact can be devastating.

PROBATE COURT

From the perspective of most individuals, one of the most costly, time-consuming, and inconvenient systems of court in the United States is the Probate Court system. In defense of this area of law, the probate court is designed to protect people who cannot protect themselves. A minor is protected via guardianship, an adult is protected via conservatorship, and a deceased person is protected via the probate process.

When someone passes away, a probate case is opened in the court, and a judge will determine the ultimate outcome and disposition of the deceased's property. Any creditor that is owed will be paid from the estate, and any debts that are owed to the estate will be collected. Accountings, fact determinations, appraisals, and estate details will be gathered and distributed based on the will. In the absence of a valid legal will, the court will dispose of the assets according to the state's intestate disposition rules. Intestate means a person died without a known legal will.

The probate process requires a case filing fee, court-appointed reporting and oversight, executor fees, and attorney fees, which are usually nonnegotiable. In most states, a reasonable expectation of probate-related costs would be between 3% and 8% of the gross fair market estate value. Your time delays could be expected to be 12 to 20 months or longer.

Planning for the Blended Family

Jill suddenly got the worst news of her life as she stood in the doorway of the home she grew up in. This was the home in which she had raised her children. This was the home in which she had fond memories of baking with her grandmother.

She stood in the doorway, reading the letter. It was a letter from an attorney giving her 90 days to leave the home that had been in her family for several generations. Her grandparents bought it when they married. Her mom grew up in the home. And Jill had grown up there and raised her children there. They now had a matter of weeks to vacate the premises due to the law.

Jill's father, Dan, had passed away in his 40s. When that occurred, Jill's mother, Sue, moved into a condo, and Jill and her husband moved back "home" to continue raising their family. Later, her mother remarried. Over the course of time, Jill's mother died. Because Jill's mother and stepfather had not created a trust that kept the family home in the family, when Jill's stepfather died, his children decided to sell the property and evict Jill's family from the residence.

With no legal recourse, Jill and her husband were forced to leave their home and would not be receiving any value from the property; and to add insult to injury, all their household furniture and furnishings were to be sold by her stepbrothers at a yard sale.

What Sue could have done differently was create a Living or Asset Protection Trust with her second husband, which would have assured that their wishes for the home to remain in their family would be carried out. Sadly, because they did not put a trust in place, the outcome was detrimental to Sue's family and her grandchildren and their legacy.

As an additional note, Jill's stepbrothers had to endure the cost and delays of probate court before they could take the title and evict Jill and her family. The real winners were the attorneys that handled the probate and the stepbrothers, who celebrated their unintended windfall.

Consider what would happen to your family home in the event of a death.

Is there a family conversation that should be scheduled?

Is the intention for distribution understood by all involved family members?

If the assets are not intended to be distributed "equally," have properly executed legal documents been prepared?

How could you create a legacy of improved family harmony by planning ahead?

FAMILY COURT

For parents of minor children, the welfare of the children is a natural part of parental desire and responsibility. When family life activities are progressing as planned and parents are living happy, healthy lives, there is no issue. The problems often occur when an unexpected health issue, accident, or death occurs. Then what happens to the young children?

For the protection of minors, the court will not allow a relative or friend to take custody in such an event absent the parent's consent. If a parent is alive and well and can give permission for relatives to temporarily care for the children, it will be allowed. If the parent is unable to give such permission, whether through death or incapacitation, without a written legal document, children will be whisked away to foster care and often separated in the event of their parent's accident or serious health event. This can be the result if one or both parents are killed or seriously injured.

A legal, formal, and updated will is the document that provides detailed instructions for custody and care of minor children. For a long-term solution, a living trust will provide the person the parents have chosen as a trustee with the financial means and instructions for the health, education maintenance, and support of minor children.

Preparing your Legacy Plan to avoid a foster care mandate or the need for family court intervention should be a priority if you are the parent of minor children. We don't always know what will happen in life; however, we can be prepared for many contingencies. Creating a will with appropriate provisions

for minor children is a small financial and time sac-
rifice to have this area of your life in order.

You may hear that a will must be recorded in your
local county or that you need a will notarized or that
it may not be handwritten. These are myths.

Two types of valid wills exist. The first type is a
holographic will. It is a handwritten will that should
not contain any typewritten words at all. It must be
signed and dated. Do not have this document notarized, witnessed, or recorded. Doing so may invalidate your will altogether, depending on the state in
which you live. The second type of valid will is a formal will. This should be prepared by an estate attorney, and it will be witnessed by at least two qualified
witnesses. Because estate law is sensitive and specific requirements are necessary, it is not advisable
to try this on your own. For example, if one of your
two witnesses is related to you, the entire will fails in
most states.

Recording a will does not invalidate it; however, it
makes otherwise private information a matter of
public record. Anyone can find out who your family

is and what assets you own and exploit the information and relationships. To avoid potential predators and marketing trolls, do your family a favor and keep your estate planning private. A detailed description of wills is included in the "Protecting Yourself" section of this book.

PROTECTING YOUR BUSINESS

When determining the type of entity under which to operate your business, your most important considerations will be costs, taxation, formalities, and liability.

CORPORATIONS

There are two types of corporations, C Corporation and S Corporation. Both issue stock to shareholders, who own the company. Each corporation is operated by elected directors, who are elected by the shareholders. As profits are declared, the dividends are paid to the shareholders according to the number of owned shares. Corporations are required by law to maintain records, pay annual fees, file reports with the state of domicile (or residence), keep minutes of regular meetings, issue stock, and follow the corporate bylaws.

The advantage of a corporation is the protection from personal liability that it provides. Because it is a separate entity from its owners, the personal assets of each stockholder are not at risk, nor are they subject to corporate debts. It is important to note that failure to uphold corporate formalities may cause a "piercing of the corporate veil" and eliminate the liability protection. Be diligent in your implementation of all formalities in order to reap the benefits of either type of corporation.

The primary distinction between a C corporation and an S corporation is the federal taxation treatment. C corporation profits are taxed as they are reported on the IRS Corporation Tax Return. Any after-tax profits are distributed to the shareholders. Upon receiving dividends, C corporation shareholders are taxed on their personal tax returns. This is often considered a double tax.

By contrast, dividends distributed to shareholders of an S corporation are taxed only once, as they are paid out to shareholders. The shareholders are usually officers and directors of the corporation. The S corporation must have fewer than 100 shareholders, issue only one class of stock, and be owned by United States citizens or residents. The advantage of choosing an S corporation is having tax savings while enjoying liability protection. An S corporation owner may pass through losses against other personal income or gains that occur in the same year. This means that losses that the owner incurs from his business can be "written off" against his other salary or earned income.

An advantage of a C corporation is the ability to control the flow of dividends in order to maintain cash reserves and operating capital.

For state tax purposes, most states also pass profits and losses through to S corporation shareholders. Like with federal corporate taxes, some states impose a double taxation structure for C corporations.

LIMITED LIABILITY CORPORATIONS (LLC) AND LIMITED LIABILITY PARTNERSHIPS (LLP)

When choosing the most appropriate and beneficial business entity between a Limited Liability Corporation (LLC) and a Limited Liability Partnership (LLP), the determining factors will include management requirements, liability protections, tax benefits, and business insurance requirements.

An LLC is a company with the taxation benefits of a partnership and the liability protection of a corporation. Unlike other corporations, the shareholders may be domestic or foreign entities, other LLCs, corporations, or individuals. Some states require professional corporations, such as physicians, dentists, accountants, attorneys, and architects, to create a Professional Limited Liability Company (PLLC), rather than an LLC.

An LLP is a general partnership created by two or more partners. The managing partner must be designated to be responsible for corporate liabilities, while silent partners receive liability protection for their personal assets. The scope of financial liability for LLC and LLP owners varies from state to state.

The IRS treats an LLP favorably by passing through earnings to the partners. Each partner is responsible for reporting profits and losses on their personal tax returns. An informational tax return is required by the IRS each year for both an LLC and an LLP. In some states, certain types of LLCs are required to file as a corporation rather than a partnership.

Please use your financial planner, tax attorney, and tax planning experts to help you optimize your business entity options. In most cases, you may change your business entity if you are not currently enjoying the benefits of your best option.

GENERAL PARTNERSHIP

A General Partnership is an appropriate business entity choice for business owners who want to share profits, losses, taxes, management, and liability. An unlimited number of partners may be joined for the business management and profits. Partnership interests may be added, reduced, or severed, subject to the legal partnership agreement that governs the business operations.

SOLE PROPRIETORSHIP

A Sole Proprietorship is a business owned by an individual, with or without a fictitious business name. The fictitious business name, or DBA (doing business as), is the business name under which the individual provides goods or services. If you own a sole proprietorship, you will receive all earnings as ordinary income. You will report your earnings to the IRS and state of domicile (residence) annually.

As a sole proprietor, you are personally responsible for any liability of your business, and you must pay self-employment tax and make social security and Medicare contributions. Regarding the raising of capital, it can be difficult due to the absence of partners, shares, and membership interests associated with a sole proprietorship. There is nothing legally transferable to provide a business investor.

For many small businesses and start-up organizations, a sole proprietorship is an appropriate and low-cost first step. Once your business has the capital and profits to sustain working capital, tax payments, operating expenses, business licenses, and tax return preparation, it may be time to consider other business entity options. Other business entities may help reduce taxation, increase capital raising options, and reduce liability.

Schooled and Foolish

Tammie filed her tax return on her own because she was attending graduate school. She exercised the educational credit on her tax return. She completed the appropriate form and turned it in, feeling good about the $2,500 in taxes she wouldn't have to pay.

What she didn't know was that because of her income, the tax credit wouldn't apply to her level of schooling. By the time she received the IRS notice that $2,500 was actually owed, she was assessed another $1,700 in penalties and interest.

Hindsight is 20/20. What she could have done was hire a qualified tax preparer to properly file her returns. In the end, it would have saved her quite a bit of money.

PROTECTING YOURSELF

When you consider the number of choices you make daily about your personal care, lifestyle, relationships, and finances, there are many. You probably don't even think about how much control you have to make determinations about your life. Something you may want to consider is, what exactly could happen if you didn't have the ability or control to make those decisions by yourself and for yourself?

How would your wishes regarding your personal and medical care be carried out?

Who would make choices for you regarding your end-of-life dignity concerns?

Where would your assets be managed and distributed?

To whom would your wealth transfer, and how would the people or entities receive it?

It is time to explore your options for legal documents and special provisions that will help you answer these questions.

POWERS OF ATTORNEY, HEALTH CARE DIRECTIVES, AND LIVING WILLS

There are some circumstances in life that cannot be improved, even with unlimited wealth at our disposal. Many would agree that their health and freedom are more important than their wealth. How, then, can we protect ourselves when life does not go as planned?

POWER OF ATTORNEY

A Power of Attorney is a legal document that you create allowing someone to act on your behalf if you are unable. Depending on what you would like to accomplish with your power of attorney, you have four basic choices.

A General Power of Attorney is comprehensive and allows your chosen Attorney-in-Fact to sign documents, conduct financial transactions, complete contracts, and pay bills for you. Absent a formal decision, the power you delegate to another person ends only upon your death.

In contrast, a Limited Power of Attorney restricts your chosen attorney-in-fact to only act on your behalf for a specific purpose. You may need a contract or deed to be signed on a day in the future when you will be unavailable. The limited power of attorney has an end date.

A Durable Power of Attorney allows your attorney-in-fact to sign on your behalf only after a court has appointed a conservator or guardian for you.

A Springing Power of Attorney has a provision added to define the standard for determining incapacity. This document may allow your attorney-in-fact to act on your behalf without the intervention of the court.

Benefits of a Power of Attorney

Jack and Lori couldn't have been more excited for their son. Jeremy was accepted to attend his #1 choice of university and had already begun his classes. Then, on a Friday evening, they got the phone call. On the other end of the phone was a nurse at the hospital near Jeremy's university. She had bad news for the family. Apparently, Jeremy was attending a fraternity rush event on campus, and something went wrong. He had been injured and was currently in surgery.

One of Jeremy's friends was able to locate a phone number for Jeremy's parents to give to the hospital staff, which enabled them to make the call. When Lori and Jack asked for more information about the surgery, the extent of his injuries, and specifics regarding his condition, the nurse stated that she could not provide this information without a power of attorney for health care that included HIPAA language.

Weeks before he left for college, Jeremy had turned eighteen and become an adult. His parents' right to any medical information without his permission was severed. For Jack and Lori to make decisions on Jeremy's behalf, they would need to obtain permission from the court. The court would not be open until Monday morning, two days later. Without any information or details from the hospital staff (which they are prohibited from disclosing), Lori and Jack experienced several days of stress, worry, and regret.

Over time, Jeremy recovered fully and completed his studies, and the story ended well. What Jack and Lori wish they had known is that they could have created a simple power of attorney for health care that would have allowed hospital staff and physicians to share information with them as soon as he was admitted to the hospital after the accident occurred.

The result in Jeremy's case was that a pair of very concerned and freaked out parents flew across the country without knowing the condition or prognosis for their son. They dropped everything to get to him—their other children, their business, Jack's job—all to be at his bedside. The costs of dealing with the court were $3,400 and several days of distressed waiting. If Jeremy had spent more time in a coma and a conservatorship was required, costs could have been $15,000.

Because he fully recovered and resumed his studies within a couple of weeks, the greatest financial cost was merely the medical bills, rather than significant court and attorney's fees.

HEALTH DIRECTIVES AND LIVING WILLS

A Power of Attorney for Health Care, or Health Care Proxy, is a legal document that allows you to delegate someone to make medical decisions on your behalf. This document delegates the authority to another person to choose your treatment, surgery plan, facility, physician, and continuation or discontinuation of life-sustaining medical care.

An Advance Health Care Directive, also known as a Living Will, advance decision, medical directive, personal directive, or advance directive, is a legal document that allows you to communicate your wishes for medical treatment in the event that you are unable to do so personally.

The Health Care Proxy and Living Will are generally created simultaneously and can be combined into one document. In the context of a complete estate plan, the health care documents are the only estate planning documents that may be revoked or rescinded orally. In other words, if you are receiving medical treatment and your attorney-in-fact has been making medical decisions for you, you may override their decisions and your wishes will be honored.

Properly completing your health care planning documents will potentially save you a substantial amount of money by avoiding the court process of determining your incapacity or gaining court permission for another to make medical decisions on your behalf. By planning, you will also have a say in how you are treated during an incapacity, whether temporary or permanent and whether physical or mental. Your life-end dignity issues will be planned for. For example, you may instruct your caregivers to provide certain hair and nail care, wardrobe choices, and entertainment and social choices even if you are unable to communicate.

The combination of documents that determine who makes medical decisions for you and what decisions you would have them make varies from state to state. When you are updating or initially creating your health care planning documents, please rely on the advice of your estate planning attorney.

When it comes to health care power of attorney, directive to physicians, or living will, you want to understand the following risk. Creating your health care documents delegates authority to someone else to act on your behalf to deal with medical decisions and health care providers. Once your document is executed and is legally in place, please do not sign any papers when you go to the hospital for a medical procedure.

Sometimes the medical staff, although they mean well, will mistakenly require you to sign their version of directive or health care power of attorney. It's important that you do not sign one, because doing so will negate any planning done up to that moment.

Signing the paper doesn't make your planning better; it makes your planning void. Simply mention to the staff that you have planning, and if they need documents, you can arrange for them to be provided.

If you have not already created appropriate medical documents, then you should sign the medical facility's directive, because in this case, something may be better than nothing.

Avoid Simple Mistakes

Bob was scheduled for a procedure that would allow the blood in the vessels around his heart to flow more freely. Two days before surgery, he entered the hospital surgery center for a chest X-ray, lab testing, and EKG and to complete pre-operation medical paperwork.

The nice young administrator asked him to sign a series of forms, including a fill-in-the-blank health care directive form, and Bob signed the form. Besides adding his son Chip's name on top, he left the health care directive form incomplete.

Bob's procedure went as planned; however, before he was released from the hospital, he experienced complications. The hospital, in their attempt to locate Bob's son Chip, called the home phone, which was answered by Bob's younger son, Joey, who said he had the health care power of attorney available and could make decisions on Bob's behalf. Because Bob had signed the document at the hospital that specified only his son Chip, they would not talk to his son Joey. During this stressful, upsetting time, the family and medical staff had to wait eight hours for Chip to arrive before they could decide what to do and move forward with Bob's treatment.

Had Bob not signed the form and instead indicated that he had a health directive in place already, Joey could have immediately given direction to the medical staff and saved precious time.

To learn more about health care directives and living wills, visit www.JudyCopenbarger.com/truth.

Plan While You Can

Rob and Mary had concerns as Rob's parents began to age and exhibit poor health symptoms. Their estate planning became a common conversation, but they just weren't ready.

Over several years, Rob and Mary approached the subject with Samuel, Rob's dad, who did not want to jinx anything by creating an estate plan or writing a will or executing a trust or dealing with attorneys. (He didn't like attorneys, anyway.)

When Rob's mother passed away, there were business items to take care of, but the big, life-changing event for Samuel occurred one spring afternoon. Samuel was dining at a popular steakhouse during the early bird dinner seating when he began to choke on his meal. Patrons in the restaurant attempted CPR, and an ambulance arrived from the hospital down the street.

The good news and bad news … they were able to save Samuel's life. In short, Samuel functionally died that day, but he didn't physically die that day. For the next 16 months, Samuel "existed" in a conscious yet unaware state. He required a breathing tube, a feeding tube, and 24-hour care. The lights were on, but no one was home.

The extended family, his son Rob, and Mary, Rob's wife, took weekly shifts looking after Samuel and providing for his care. Because Samuel's lungs required periodic suctioning, his care costs were over $20,000 a month. Fortunately, Samuel had the retirement funds saved for most of his care.

Because Samuel had not created proper estate documents, it was not clear to the family or health care providers how to deal with his condition, termination of treatment, and end-of-life dignity concerns. It was traumatic for Samuel and his family in that the emotional, financial, spiritual, and relational aspects of their lives were forever negatively impacted.

HOLOGRAPHIC AND FORMAL WILLS

Here's the truth about wills. There are two types that are important to understand when it comes to the end of someone's life. The two types are Formal and Holographic.

A living will is not to be mistaken for a will. A living will has to do with delegating medical decisions to another person, which is totally different from a "last will and testament."

A Holographic Will is a handwritten document. For a holographic will to be accepted as a bona fide legal document, it must be signed and dated. It is best to have absolutely no typing or printing on a holographic will. This document should <u>not</u> be notarized or witnessed. It should only be created in the personal handwriting of the testator (the person who is writing it).

The other type of will is a Formal Will. A formal will has legal requirements in order to be valid and considered by the court upon someone's death. This may be typed or handwritten. It may be notarized and must be witnessed by two people who are not likely beneficiaries and are eighteen years or older.

Many people mistakenly record their wills in the county in which they live. This is not necessary and often creates more complications when someone passes away. Please do not record your formal will.

With a basic understanding of the two types of wills, your best step is to determine which will is right for you. If key language is missing from a holographic will or if the intention of the writer is not crystal clear to the court, the holographic will or provisions in this will may fail. A failed provision might mean that your assets unintentionally go to people that you didn't want to have them. It could mean that someone gets more than their share, and it could mean that someone you intended to give something to gets nothing at all.

Specific language must be included in your holographic will in order to avoid confusion or lack of clarity. Be sure to include in a handwritten or holographic will the following language:

"This is my last will and testament. I revoke all wills and prenuptials previously made by me, and I name _____ to act as my executor. Upon my death, I want the following people or charities to receive the following assets."

List your assets with the named recipients.

Sign and date this document, and you're well on your way.

If it is important to you to be sure there is nothing missing and that the people you care about receive what you'd like to leave them, you should engage an attorney, not a paralegal, to prepare a properly documented formal will for you. If your attorney specializes in estate planning or holds an LLM in estates or taxation, they would know what you need and be able to help you.

Sign and Date Your Holographic Will, Please

Paula was fortunate to live a long, beautiful life. She outlived her husband by seventeen years and died in her late 80s happy and at home. She was the mother of two children, Sarah and Ronald. Sarah was always close to her mother but later in life became influenced by someone that introduced her to a serious drug-addicted lifestyle. Until this happened, Paula had intended to leave everything equally to her son and daughter. Paula created a holographic will in her fifties that she believed would give everything equally to both kids.

In her early eighties, she rewrote her will, leaving everything to Ronald. Her intent was to allow Ronald to care for his sister without giving her funds to fuel her destructive lifestyle. Paula failed to date the last version of her will. Because the court could not determine that her second "will" was written after the original, the court for the sake of fairness gave half of her assets to Sarah and the other half to Ronald.

This was not Paula's intent, but because of a small mistake, leaving the date off the will, the outcome for the distribution of the estate went very differently from Paula's intentions. Sadly, just months after Sarah received her distribution of Paula's estate, she died of a drug overdose.

Had Paula simply signed and dated the legal updates, the outcome for Sarah may have been different. Perhaps Ronald could have helped by using the funds for Sarah's detox rather than Sarah furthering her addiction with the sudden influx of cash.

To avoid some of the pitfalls that come with relying on a holographic will, you may prefer to create a formal will. Creating a formal will with an appropriately designated attorney will probably cost you less than you think. It might surprise you to know that a formal will in almost every state will cost $500 or less.

To avoid a bad experience while creating your estate plan or legal documents, please avoid an online service, paralegal legal documents, or a do-it-your-self approach. Many companies that prepare these substandard legal documents go out of business in a short time and are banned from this practice.

Over the past several decades, many people who run these companies or provide these services have been imprisoned for their practice. You do not need to fear estate attorneys or the process of creating and customizing your legal documents, but you should be prepared and aware so you can protect yourself and your family.

An important note for you to consider is the fact that a will (either type) can handle the distribution when you die, however the court must be involved, and a probate proceeding must occur for your will to be carried out.

Revocable and Irrevocable Trusts

Many people consider the costs, delays, and incon-venience of using the court to be too great, so they bypass the judicial system's costly and cumbersome process by creating some form of trust. A qualified estate planning attorney can help you set up a trust, which does not require the court's intervention.

Regarding your choice of an attorney to help you, look for a track record of good client experiences. Some "estate attorneys" will only create wills, for the sole purpose of their own personal gain. When someone dies, an attorney will generate a fee of 5% of the value of the estate if dealing with the court through the probate system. If the same attorney helps the same family of a deceased person to administer a trust, the attorney will generate a fee of 1% of the value of the estate. For this pecuniary reason, there are some who would rather help a client create a will than enhance their planning through the use of a trust.

Another common unscrupulous practice to be aware of is the "ongoing services" law practice model. Your attorney creates your original documents for you, then requires an annual fee to update them. From time to time, there are changes in the law that may require an update, but many clients receive an annual letter stating that the law has changed so their documents must be updated to be valid, and of course there's a fee for that service. Please be cautious of a pattern requiring costly annual updates.

You may consider protecting yourself financially. After all, a lifetime of accumulated wealth is worth saving.

A trust is a contract. It is a legal document that allows you to hold assets for a certain purpose. A properly created trust provides a determination of who is in charge, what they can do, and who receives the trust assets when the trust ends.

The person or people who create the trust and fund it are called the settlors, or trustors. The managers of trust assets are called trustees. Generally, successor trustees are named so that they may act upon the death or incapacity of the initial trustee(s). The beneficiaries of the trust are those persons or entities named to receive income or assets upon a certain time or event in the future.

Although there are hundreds of types of trusts and trust provisions available to provide various solutions, the most frequently utilized trusts are revocable living trusts, asset protection trusts, charitable trusts, and tax planning trusts. To maintain simplicity, we will briefly discuss the distinction between a revocable living trust and an asset protection trust.

A Revocable Living Trust is a popular legal document used by families to accomplish five goals upon their passing. This trust type will avoid the probate process, save money, capture favorable estate tax rules, streamline the management process, and ease the distribution to beneficiaries.

An Asset Protection Trust (or Irrevocable Trust) will also avoid probate. Additional benefits and features of creating an asset protection trust include your ability to protect your trust assets from creditors, predators, and long-term care expenses.

Here's what you need to know. A properly created and funded asset protection trust with specific provisions will provide you protection from future liabilities, including a failed business, an accident for which you are held liable (or allegedly liable), and ongoing health care expenses.

Having the ability to protect your assets can make all the difference when it comes to leaving a legacy for your family members, sustaining a closely held business, or ensuring financial solvency of a surviving spouse. If a lifetime of wealth accumulation is exhausted in a few years of ongoing health care, the surviving spouse may become insolvent or be forced to rely on family or the government in later years.

If you are in a business with a propensity for high-target liability, such as rental property, contracting or building, or a medical or dental profession, then you would be well-advised to consider your options for asset protection trusts and estate planning. Reach out to an estate planning attorney who specializes in asset protection trusts. Most attorneys, even some estate and tax attorneys, do not have this expertise, so please choose your legal professional wisely.

Don't Be Swindled

John and Margaret attended a free dinner seminar to learn about avoiding estate tax. The provider of the workshop introduced them to the concept of estate planning and the use of costly annuities and legal documents to reposition their assets. John and Margaret trusted the presenters of the seminar and believed that they were protecting their family by engaging their services.

Although they felt pressured to sign up immediately while in the meeting and felt the costs were extremely high, they were ultimately convinced this was the right thing to do. They felt compelled to sign the documents, although they weren't completely sure what they were.

Four years later, when John passed away, Margaret contacted the company listed on the card, only to learn that years before, the company went out of business and two of the owners were nowhere to be found. A third owner was discovered to be in prison, doing time for fraud.

After consulting an attorney, Margaret learned that the accounts they had set up to be protected had been assigned to the owners of the company and that their estate documents were never formally executed or properly funded. Her home had actually been transferred to the people with which she and John had signed the documents. Not only was Margaret emotionally devastated to learn this news, but the financial and taxation effects were profound and long-lasting.

To learn about more ways to protect your home, investments, and business, visit www.Judy Copenbarger.com/truth.

CHAPTER 5

HOW CASHFLOW PLANNING
BRINGS FINANCIAL FREEDOM

Cashflow Management is the simplest fundamental pillar of finance to improve on.

This aspect of personal and small business finance is the most active. For most, there are daily choices to be made about money. Some days, many choices need to be made about where the money should go.

You may have learned about your cashflow management, allocations, and reserves through your life experiences. Most people do. How much should I save? How much should I spend? How much should I give? Which goals should be my most important?

Pay Yourself First

Don't do anything based on fear or greed.

The Turners were referred to our offices by a friend of theirs who had experienced our Strategic Financial Planning program.

When we began working together, they were both employed in San Diego, California, at a high level, as both had graduate degrees. They had an infant daughter and were considering adopting another child.

They both were raised in homes by parents who believed in saving money in the bank. Neither of them had ever invested in real estate, stocks, bonds, or alternatives. They both were considering participation in their company-offered retirement investment accounts but were unclear how they might benefit from them.

One of the first principles they began to apply to their finances with us was "pay yourself first." The idea is to make sure that taxes are paid and that before paying expenses each month, you pay yourself money for future goals and eventual cashflows.

They began investing in themselves by contributing to their employer retirement programs, which also created substantial income tax relief for them. Within two years of substantial contributions and investments outside of their work programs, they were well on their way to achieving their most important goals. They also gained a clear understanding of all of their investment accounts, diversification principles, and reduction of risk.

For the Turners, making these changes in their financial strategic activities allowed them to make decisions based on information and sound advice rather than fear or greed.

Most investment advisers, bankers, wire houses, and financial institutions will advise clients to act out of a sense of fear or greed. They will tell stories of fear designed to lead a client to believe that if they do not act, invest, or buy a financial product within a certain timeline, then they will lose something.

The other aspect of this approach is to activate the greed in a client and appeal to their desire to earn more, attain an unrealistic return, or somehow beat the system to get what they want faster and better.

The fear-and-greed sales approach is rampant in the financial world and is something to beware of when you're preparing to make an investment.

Ask yourself … is my decision based on fear or greed? Is the sales representative encouraging me to make my decision based on fear or greed? Answering these questions honestly and at the appropriate time can save you the majority of the mistakes most people make about their money.

Cashflow Planning Avoids Taxation Overwhelm

The Olivers own a successful window and fencing company. Dan is in charge of technical work and heads up the job design and manages the workers. Diane runs the office staff and makes sure all the jobs are done on time and the bills are paid.

During the first ten years of their business, they struggled with record keeping and were surprised each year by the process for income taxation. As a result, they incurred tax penalties year after year. As 1099 employees (self-employed), they were responsible for paying their own income tax and estimated taxes each quarter.

Until we sat down together to implement a strategy to make timely and appropriate tax payments, they found their business and personal taxation to be a chore and a very negative activity for them. We implemented a plan to archive a percentage of each accounts receivable as it was received. In other words, if there was $1000 remaining after expenses and labor were paid, then 30% would go into a savings account for taxes and 20% would go into future growth of the business. In this example, $300 goes to tax and $200 to marketing and development and acquiring new customers.

For the past eight years, the Olivers have always had excess funds for capitalizing the business, growing their customer base and making a lot of money, which now is funding their goals for future retirement and travel. More importantly, they're not stressed about taxes, and they always have enough, even with increased profits, to pay taxes fully and on time.

If you are a 1099 employee or are self-employed, you might consider saving a percentage of each amount of income as received. Your percentage can be estimated by adding state tax rate to your estimated federal tax rate. A good starting range for taxes is 30–50%. If you are in the client or customer acquisition phase of your business, you might consider depositing 10–20% of each influx of income into an account earmarked for advertising and development.

The Olivers have put to good use all of the money that used to go to taxation penalties. They invested in their daughter's business and taught her the same principles they learned. Now their daughter happily pays herself first and allocates each month a percentage of her income to save for future taxes and to advertise her business.

Defend Against Overspending

Patrick is a dentist and has been in practice for 25 years. His wife, Karen, used to work in the office and has decided to spend time helping their children care for their own families. She enjoys taking the babies to the park and to the zoo and, to his dismay, to the mall. Frankly … she shops too much!

When they asked us how they could get a handle on overspending, we helped them with a spending plan to allow for flexibility and spontaneity but keep them within their plan. Her habit was to spend whatever was in their personal expense account, and in between pay periods she would spend it down to zero every time.

Once they implemented "the secret," they were able to accumulate cash reserves, maintain their expense accounts, and save substantially more for their future. This is "the secret" they implemented: We recommended they open a savings account at a bank two cities away, and each pay period her instructions were to make a deposit to that savings account before spending any money. This account did not have a checking account attached to it. It did not have ATM privileges. As a result, the savings became true savings for them.

The tension around their family financial conversations disappeared, and their marital harmony increased. They are grateful to have such staggering results from such a simple savings strategy. Perhaps a savings account that is not convenient to access could be helpful for you as well. Put the SAVE back in SAVINGS.

To access more ways to improve your marital harmony around money, visit www.JudyCopenbarger.com/truth.

INCOME AND EXPENSES

Managing the reserves and flow of cash consists of a series of small choices that you will make almost daily. Having a plan that directs your daily choices can be life-changing. If you make decisions about your money with intention, you can anticipate the outcome of your planning.

Start with your income. Once you determine the gross total of monthly household revenue that you must work with, subtract your taxes and gifting. The remaining monthly balance is the amount you have left to allocate to living expenses, savings, and future goals.

A common mistake is to forget to allow for special gifts, travel, clothing, vacations, and other irregular expenses. For example, you may enjoy giving birthday, holiday, and hospitality gifts throughout the year. You may spontaneously help someone in need or plan some travel. Irregular expenses are those that you do not pay monthly, but they can be expected. Examples of irregular expenses are real estate taxes, insurance premiums, debt services, and automobile and home repairs. You know you will have these expenses, but you may not necessarily plan for them in your monthly expense plan.

ESCROW ACCOUNT

Consider opening an Escrow Account for the known and unexpected irregular expenditures. You will allocate a certain amount of money each month to this account, so when nonmonthly expenses are due, you are prepared to make the payment. To determine your monthly deposit into your escrow account, add up your annual estimates of the non-monthly expenses and divide the annual amount by twelve. Saving this amount each month will help you avoid most financial surprises and avoid the expense of using consumer credit to make ends meet.

Withdrawals from your escrow account, cash reserves, and other goal-focused savings accounts should only occur when it is time to pay an expense or fund a goal. If you need help maintaining your savings as savings, you might consider having your savings accounts at a separate bank from your cash-flow and expense accounts. Perhaps your savings accounts could be in an inconvenient location or another city, with no ATM capability. Create specific goals for each account. How much will be in this reserve account? By what date will I achieve that goal?

At a minimum, your Cash Reserves account should contain an amount that would cover three or four months of basic monthly expenses. If you sleep better at night with six or more months of expense coverage, then that is your number. If you currently do not consistently have that amount in savings, then set a goal to achieve it in the coming months. The peace of mind this reserve will give you is invaluable.

With an escrow account fully funded for upcoming expenses and cash reserves at an appropriate level, it is time to create and implement a monthly spending plan.

SPENDING PLAN

Create a list of your monthly Fixed Expenses. These are the amounts with payments that rarely change. Examples may include your mortgage or rent payment, utilities and phone, auto payments, memberships, subscriptions, and monthly insurance premiums. Then, add to your list an itemization of your monthly Variable Expenses. Examples will include food, gas, grooming, medical and fitness, and entertainment.

Separating fixed from variable expenses will help you adjust your spending plan when you come up short. You may be aware that surprises in life can often come in batches. Have you ever had the experience of updating the garbage disposal, replacing your car tires, celebrating three special occasions, and hosting unexpected company within a tight time frame? It all happens at once sometimes, doesn't it?

Using a Spending Plan Template will help you stay on track with your expenses. You will find an example in the appendix.

Your peace of mind and sense of security will increase as you achieve your goals of fully funding your cash reserves and escrow account. Purposefully approaching each month with a spending plan will provide structure, which many people interpret as freedom. It has been said that when your vision is clear, your decisions are easy. Following your template while making your daily spending and savings choices will bring you a new financial confidence.

How to Reposition Debt and Pay It Off Fast

When the Vickers were six years from their planned retirement date, they decided to put their financial house in order. Dean is a professor at a prestigious university in Texas, and Sue is a supervising nurse at a local hospital.

The first thing they did was assess their current investments accounts, debt accounts, and goal funding requirement amounts. Because they had $127,000 in personal consumer debt, we advised them to borrow a line of credit against their home to pay off their credit cards and their car loans. The interest rate on their auto loan was 7.2%, and the interest rates on their credit cards ranged from 16.5% to 24.9%.

By repositioning their debt, they were able to save $600 per month in interest costs and entirely pay off their debts within the year. The money they saved in interest and consumer debt became cashflow, and they were able to fund that additional cashflow into their escrow account. Their escrow account is earmarked for their most important goals.

Included in these goals is the purchase of their next car in four years, for which they will pay cash; an anniversary trip to Paris; and a theme park vacation with their grandchildren. The escrow account, named "Freedom Account," receives $1,800 monthly to fund these goals for them. It is automatically transferred to their escrow account from their checking account each time they receive a paycheck.

Here are your Debt Repayment Strategies. This is good stuff! There are three ways to approach a debt repayment strategy.

(1) Pay highest interest rates first.

(2) Choose the consumer credit accounts with the smallest balances to pay first.

(3) Pay *pro rata*, all excess cash each month is allocated to each consumer debt account, by percentage of total debt.

Each of these strategies works. Pick one, set a goal, and be consistent. Your debt will be paid off surprisingly quickly. Your choices for a Debt Repayment Strategy can be found in the Appendix of this book.

The unsaid truth here is that you can't add more debt as you pay it off. You need to consider a cash method of expenses for this to be sustainably successful.

If you are challenged with your debt repayment strategy and want to efficiently eliminate your entire debt, visit www.JudyCopenbarger.com/truth.

Establish Appropriate Cash Reserves

In order to properly organize their savings, the Vickers implemented a two-part approach. Because at this time, their cash reserve was inadequate, they allocated all their excess monthly income toward cash reserves, and short-term goals. They determined that their cash reserves should represent four months of their expected monthly expenses, so it was necessary to fill their cash reserves before fully funding their other goals. They settle into an ongoing allocation of 60% excess cash to cash reserves and the remaining 40% to short-term goals.

Once cash reserves are fully funded (four months' basic expenses), then the excess cash allocation goes to 40% short-term, 40% mid-range, and 20%

long-term. Short-term is a goal achieved in under two years. Mid-range goals are achieved in three to five years, and long-term goals take six years or more.

For example, if you are planning to purchase a new car in four years, that would be a mid-range goal. Retirement in 11 years is a long-term goal.

Your escrow account is a simple checking or savings account you open at your favorite credit union or banking institution for the purpose of saving for future goals. Note that the cash allocated to your escrow account is cash in excess of your fixed and flexible ordinary monthly expenses.

CHAPTER 6

How to Grow & Protect Your Assets for Today & Tomorrow

Asset Management is the fundamental pillar of finance that most people think of when they consider their financial circumstances. This area includes Business Interests, Real Estate, and Investments.

To better understand your asset values and opportunities, let's explore some of the asset management basics.

BUSINESS INTERESTS

Business owners either have managers to handle business operations or manage the day-to-day operations personally. For many people, the greatest portion of their net worth is the value of the family business or closely held corporation.

In the "Protecting Your Business" section of this book, you will discover valuable strategies to protect your business by properly choosing and managing your business entities. Understanding the taxation, legacy and liability issues for each business entity is an essential element of growing family wealth through your business interests.

REAL ESTATE

Real estate is a substantial portion of net worth for many people in the United States. Beyond home-ownership, a real estate portfolio may include business-related real estate, commercial investments, and residential rentals. The greatest advantages of a realty portfolio are the increase in property values and the potential for ongoing cashflow. The downsides are the potential tort liabilities and annual taxation.

INVESTMENTS

If you have participated in an employer retirement program, individual retirement account, brokerage account, or individual investment portfolio, you understand the value of Asset Growth. The big goal is to allow your money to make you more money over time.

Cash-based investments are either qualified or non-qualified. They are either equity-based, interest-based, or insurance-based. These are the most fundamental principles for you to understand about your investments.

QUALIFIED OR NON-QUALIFIED INVESTMENTS

The characterization of your Qualified Investment accounts stems from the tax-deferral nature of them. These funds are invested before they are taxed and will grow without any income tax due until the funds are withdrawn. The IRS provides for qualified investments of funds that are contributed to retirement programs. Examples include 401(k), 457, 403(b), individual retirement accounts, deferred compensation programs, and a variety of other employer-offered retirement programs.

Non-Qualified Investment funds are invested after taxes have been paid on the income. They do not qualify for any level of tax-deferred or tax-exempt status. Tax is due on non-qualified investment accounts annually.

EQUITY INVESTMENTS

Equity-Based Investments are funded into stocks, real property, or alternatives that are owned by the investor. The goal for equity investments is for them to grow; however, the risk of loss is usually on the investor. In general, the more market risk the investor accepts, the more potential for growth they will receive. Equity investments also share a characteristic of growth-related revenue, such as dividends and ongoing returns. These investments may be qualified or non-qualified.

INTEREST INVESTMENTS

Interest-Based Investments consist of interest-related instruments. Common examples of interest-based investments are commercial paper, certificates of deposit, bonds, treasury notes, and treasury bills. In general, the investor "loans" funds to the government, a municipality, or a corporation in order to receive an agreed-upon interest rate. Interest instruments are funded for a set period, during which the investor receives the income percentage. Historically, returns on interest investments have been used to reduce market risk in a portfolio or to create a reliable income stream. These investments may be qualified or non-qualified.

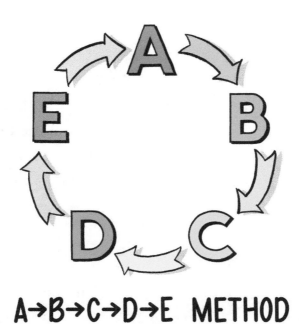

A→B→C→D→E METHOD

5 Steps to Successful Investing

Assess → Balance → Connect → Deliver → Evaluate

Tom and Terri Nelson recently retired after receiving a substantial inheritance from a family member who passed away.

Tom is a licensed contractor in the State of Connecticut, and Terri recently retired from an in-home health care placement office. They both love to travel and expect to spend four months a year abroad, starting this year.

Step 1: Assess

To invest their inheritance, they followed the five steps to successful investing, starting with step 1, Assessment. The assessment portion of the process provided insights to the resources available, the taxation implications, and their actual sustainable cashflow.

Step 2: Balance

Once these numbers were determined, Tom and Terri moved ahead to step 2, Balance. I worked with them to balance their desired outcome from their investable assets with my recommendations based on risk tolerance, horizon, sustainability, and risk management.

Step 3: Connect

Once we agreed on the desired goals of their investment, they moved to step 3, Connect. In this phase of planning, together we connected their dollars with resources, investment vehicles, and products that would optimize the growth and protection of their investable assets. Real estate, business interests, legacy documents, mutual funds, stocks, bonds, and insurance products rounded out their portfolio to meet their needs and fund their goals.

Step 4: Deliver

In this portion of the process, the monies are invested and growing. For the Nelsons, delivery occurred when their insurance policies and annuities were issued, when their mutual funds were selected, and when their stock and bond portfolio was fully allocated.

Step 5: Evaluate

The Nelsons revisit their allocations and investment performance on a quarterly basis to ensure their investments are meeting their ongoing needs and can meet their goals. If there are gaps or underperformance, a reallocation of their current model can be considered and, if necessary, implemented.

What steps to success need the most improvement in your financial life?

Are there any steps you have failed to include in the past?

What is the most important step for you to add, change, or eliminate in your current Strategic Financial Planning?

Did you notice that the 5 Steps begin with the letters A-B-C-D-E? As you plan, this will help you remember to include each step, in order.

Emotional Investing Curve

Observe the masses, and do the opposite. Don't buy high and sell low.

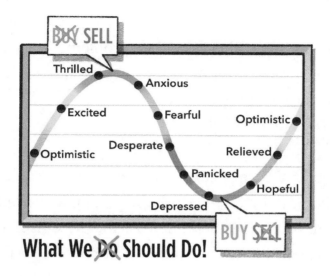

What We ~~Do~~ Should Do!

Jorge and Sylvia Reyes and their family live in Oregon. They have five school-age children. Sylvia is not interested in finance and is happy to have Jorge be in charge of their personal finances, tax return, organization, and retirement planning. She doesn't want to learn about money and finds the subject to be intimidating.

Jorge has very little formal financial education and has learned most of what he knows from his friends and acquaintances. He tends to implement his financial activities by cloning what other people are doing. When people are buying a particular technology stock, financial stock, or investment, he is known to do the same. The problem with Jorge's approach is that by the time he takes action, it has seriously cost him.

Here's how …

When "XYZ" tech stock has a low price, people are reluctant to invest, because the price may be reflective of the actual stock value. As the price rises, psychologically, people want to "wait and see." After a substantial rise in price, people become interested, and consequently the stock rises more.

Cyclically, the stock price falls, and as it does, we become aware and become increasingly concerned. Once Jorge actually takes action about the concern regarding his falling stock, the stock has fallen significantly, and he sells at a low price. He bought high and sold low based on his personal, emotional decision-making processes.

We don't want to buy high and sell low. Instead, we want to buy low and sell high. Unfortunately, most novice investors like Jorge make the mistake of following their emotional state rather than objectively purchasing and redeeming holdings based on actual value and realistic projections.

Don't be like Jorge! Once Sylvia learned about the emotional investment cycle, she realized how Jorge had been choosing poorly in buying and selling their stock. When Jorge changed his stock timing and purchase patterns, Silvia was grateful, and she realized in the long run how they'd be much better off for what they'd learned.

INSURANCE INVESTMENTS

Insurance-Based Investments may be invested into equities, interest instruments, or cash investments. An insurance company will create and manage the investments while offering certain guarantees. The guarantees include death benefits, living needs benefits, longevity protection, guaranteed income, or guaranteed principal protection. Because insurance company contracts have such diversity in their offerings, it is important to understand the nature of the offering and study each contract's benefits, features, and restrictions.

Examples of interest-based investments include whole life insurance, universal life insurance, indexed permanent insurance, variable annuities, indexed annuities, and fixed annuities. These investments may be qualified or non-qualified.

MUTUAL FUNDS

You may choose Mutual Funds for your retirement investments or individual growth accounts. A mutual fund is a collection of stocks, bonds, or both. Mutual funds provide a simple way to diversify into many sectors of investment and hedge market risk with interest instruments. Mutual funds are rated for their returns, risks, and costs. Because returns, risks, and costs vary greatly among the thousands of mutual fund offerings, you would be well-advised to seek the advice of a financial planner to help you properly allocate your investments.

To optimize your asset management, be sure to consider all genres of investment. Your perfect allocation of investments, growth assets, and income-producing holdings may not look like that of your friend, neighbor, or relative. The variables of risk tolerance, time horizon, money beliefs, financial experiences, and goals will all impact your decision-making and optimal asset allocation.

INVESTMENT STRATEGIES

How to Find a Reliable Professional

Truth is, unfortunately, there is an ongoing trend among unscrupulous professionals in the financial industry who might tend to prioritize their personal gain above your best interest. Realizing this statement does not apply to all financial professionals, it raises the question: How would you know which professionals are going to serve you and which professionals will serve their own interests?

Here's how you can create a short list of professionals that are less likely to have a conflict of interest.

Work with financial professionals with appropriate credentials. Look for these three things:

(1) Do they have a BA degree in finance or business or a certified financial planner designation? This means that, at a minimum, they have completed formal college education.

(2) Do they have an accredited investment fiduciary credential? This means the governing law requires them to act in your best interest rather than in the interest of their commission or gain.

(3) Does your financial professional engage you for a professional fee? This means you are more likely to receive appropriate advice, because they are working for you rather than for institutions paying a commission to sell products.

These three screening devices can help you make a smarter choice when determining whose advice you want to implement.

Whenever you can remove a natural conflict of interest with someone who is in sales, you will position yourself better. I'm not saying sales people, products, or advice are bad. What I am saying is that there are ways to minimize abuses and predatory behavior from professionals if you keep your eyes open and are diligent. Always ask yourself the following … "How is this advice good for me? How is it good for them?"

The biggest red flag for predatory behavior is the hurry to buy, act, invest. If you're feeling pressure, run. What they don't know is, if they treat you like a meal ticket, you're going to feel like food. Next time you feel like food, just reread this story:

Is Do-It-Yourself Investing Right for You?

Jim Williams is a high school math teacher. His wife, Val, has been married to him long enough to know, "Jim knows everything," just ask him. He will verify and clarify and terrify anyone who stands in the way of his finding the truth.

The problem is that when he gets to the truth, it isn't always. When Val's father passed away, he left her a substantial inheritance. It was more money than either of them had ever seen, because they had always lived frugally. They had been planning to depend on Jim's pension when he retired from teaching.

Jim decided to invest their money online with a discount online trading service company. He was confident that he was paying no fees, incurring no costs, and receiving only the best advice generated by his "robo" investment platform. After a couple of years of Jim self-managing their millions and losing a substantial portion of it, Val encouraged him to seek the advice and counsel of a professional.

He finally humbled himself and sought help. They learned the actual cost of the trading platform and costs of making trades themselves, which opened their eyes to the true cost of wire houses and commercial retail financial institutions like the bank's sales force.

When they wanted to buy a holding, such as a stock, although the stock price changes constantly every day, the highest price would be applied upon their purchase. If they were selling a holding, the lowest price would be applied. The difference was the increase margin, which was retained by the online trading service company.

Val and Jim realized they were increasingly receiving emails and pop-up alerts that would direct them to place trades. These alerts may have come in the form of well-meaning advice. But many of the trades resulted in both short- and long-term substantial losses for Val and Jim.

Val was extremely unhappy to learn that every time they bought and sold some stock, the company gained money and they lost money. There was also the annoying informational drip of reminders and timing tips to buy this stock and sell that stock. The company was constantly trying to upsell them new and improved tip services.

That particular company supposedly focused on selling the good investment to and buying the bad investment from them. When an online services company is also a dealer, they are selling their inventory to clients and buying inventory from clients. It is in the best interest of the company to buy increasing value stocks and sell decreasing value stocks.

So, ask yourself … what is the incentive for daily advice?

Anytime you are buying or selling a stock or any holding in your portfolio, you should have several good reasons for doing so. Ask yourself the following questions:

- How's the company doing?

- How's the sector?

- Who is the CEO?

- Who are the management advisers?

- What's their plan for future operations?

- What's the projection in their market products and services?

- How profitable is the company?

- What's the current debt structure?

Having a basic understanding of these important issues will help you direct a decision to buy or sell based on sound information. If you were buying a company, what would you ask about it before doing so? The same should be asked even if you are buying only a small portion of shares. Generic advice received via electronic transmission from a sales firm is not going to be best for you and your family.

LADDERING

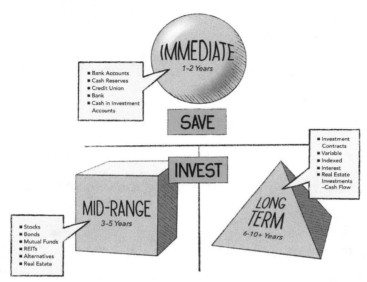

LADDERING

Anytime you are determining how to save or invest your money, you can rely on the process of Laddering, as it is discussed here.

In the world of finance, the concept of laddering originates from the consideration of timing. It has to do with the maturity or horizon of an investment and the benefit of "diversification" using various time frames. For example, for an investment of $1,000, in order to reduce risk, it would be better to invest $100 each month in 10 accounts in a 12-month Certificate of Deposit than to invest the entire $1,000 at once. With the monthly approach, there will be 10 opportunities to improve the interest rate using the laddering strategy of $100 per month of investment.

So here's how you can benefit from the concept of Laddering and an intentional approach to investing your money.

First, decide when you will need the funds you are investing. You always have a horizon, and you will want to plan for NOW, SOON, and LATER.

Your "NOW" money is cash that should be saved rather than invested. Your savings belongs in cash stored in a safety deposit box or on your personal residence or business premises. Your cash could also be saved in a credit union or bank or in a money market account. A Money Market Account is a cash account that may earn more than a passbook savings account when interest rates have a good margin.

The amount of money you keep in savings should equal your emergency fund and any money you will need to fund a financial goal or make an expenditure within the next one to two years.

Please note that your immediate or "NOW" money is not invested, and it remains above the line in your Laddering Diagram. Now, let's look below the line.

Your "SOON" money is cash that should be invested and working for you rather than sitting in a credit union or bank, earning money for that institution. This money should be growing for your use and enjoyment. Included in your "SOON" money are purchases, goals, or expenses that you expect to fund within three to five years from now. We would call this a mid-range horizon for each goal. You may intend to purchase a car, invest in some housing, or pursue education or travel within that time frame.

Once you determine how much money you will need for your extraordinary expenses and goals three to five years from now, add up the total and fund those investment choices, with liquidity as a substantial feature. These are funds you can readily get your hands on when you find that perfect car, house, or travel adventure. Some investment choices with liquidity include stocks, bonds, mutual funds, short-term real estate, and alternatives.

Your "LATER" money is cash that should be invested and working for you, similar to your "SOON" money. The distinction, however, is that your long-term investments, when possible, should have a limited exposure to market risk. This is investment money that you can't afford to risk losing.

Investment Contracts are where you will find the guarantees. In these types of contracts, the company with which you are investing assumes the risks of market loss, income earnings, or your longevity, among others. Simply stated, you are promised, by contract, certain guarantees, and the guarantees vary from contract to contract. They are not all the same, by any means.

General Investment Contracts are distinguished by the method of earnings for you. The contract may grow based on a guaranteed interest, such as a Certificate of Deposit (CD) at your credit union or bank. The contract may have an underlying portfolio of stocks and bonds and a guarantee of a minimum earning should the market underperform in any given year. The contract may guarantee a credit each year based on the performance of a Market Index, such as the S&P 500.

Your most important decisions when investing are to choose what the money will be for, when you need it, and whether liquidity or safety is most important. Using this laddering process and referring to the Laddering Diagram will help you navigate the complicated world of investing.

To learn more about laddering and download your personal Laddering Worksheet, visit www.Judy Copenbarger.com/truth.

CHAPTER 7

HOW TO REDUCE FINANCIAL
RISKS WITH INSURANCES

Insurance Planning is the fundamental pillar of finance that provides protection against various risks.

Although the growth of family assets and small businesses is an essential element of creating wealth, when it is unprotected, you could be putting it all at risk.

To better understand some of the insurances that could protect you while you are accumulating and distributing wealth, let's explore some insurance basics.

PROPERTY AND CASUALTY

Property and Casualty are types of insurance that protect your tangible property, real property, and risks associated with liability.

In this genre of insurance, you will find coverage for losses related to your belongings in the event of a covered accident. If your automobile or personal property is damaged or stolen due to a covered event or accident, you will be reimbursed for the loss. Insurance contracts may contain exemptions, deductibles, and limitations on the claims benefits you will receive in the event of a loss.

Liability Insurance covers you if you are the cause of damage to someone else's property or person. If you are covered, an insurance company will pay funds to "make whole" a person for whom your actions have caused a covered loss.

BUSINESS INSURANCE

Business insurances cover losses in the areas of property and casualty, professional liability, and incidents of loss associated with employees.

General Liability Insurance protects a business owner or corporation from a variety of claims, including property damage, personal injury, advertising injury, failed product operations, medical payments, and theft.

HEALTH INSURANCE

Health Insurance is the most complicated, ever-changing, and difficult-to-navigate area of insurance. It seems that as soon as you get a handle on it, the rules and offerings change again.

Health insurance types are categorized into three basic categories. Indemnity Coverage is the traditional insurance plan, with which you may be familiar. This coverage applies to all covered medical expenses, with the following exceptions:

Your Deductible is the amount that you pay before the insurance coverage applies. The Coinsurance is your percentage of any covered medical expenses after the deductible has been met. There is an annual Out-of-Pocket Limit that protects you from expenses beyond a certain level. Finally, the entire health insurance policy will have a stop-loss at a very high limit, such as one million dollars.

Major medical plans are often underwritten by groups and employers. Often, employers will use optimal health insurance to attract and sustain employees.

A Health Savings Account (HSA) allows qualifying individuals to make tax-deductible contributions to their account each year and use the funds for medical expenses. This provides a tax-deductible method for funding deductibles, premiums, and uncovered medical expenses. This is a huge value for those who qualify. You may have an HSA offering at your place of employment. Inquire with your human resources department or company manager to determine whether this program is available or if they would consider starting one for employees where you work.

Medicare is a government health insurance plan that covers people who are disabled or are over the age of 65. It is financed through a Medicare payroll tax, which is divided between employers and employees.

The basic provisions of Medicare are categorized into four parts:

A: Hospital Insurance, Skilled Nursing, Home Health Services

B: Medical Insurance, Diagnostics, Physician Services, Outpatient Services

C: Medicare Advantage Plans, HMOs, and PPOs

D: Outpatient Prescription Drug Coverage

Medicaid is a federal insurance program designed to provide benefits for those desperately in need. The federal government funds the programs of individual states to provide nursing home and skilled facility coverage after the 90 days covered by Medicare.

When you are exploring your insurance needs, seek the advice of your financial planner to discover your options. You should consider the following questions:

For this specific type of insurance, do you need it at all?

If so, how much coverage do you need and what can you afford?

Is there a more direct and less expensive way to obtain this insurance?

What options do you have?

Is there another way you can mitigate this risk without paying premiums?

While an insurance agent will be versed in the benefits and features of certain insurance contracts, they may not be trained in the overall fit of the policy into your life. In considering cashflows, risk tolerances, your personal history and preferences, taxation issues, and legacy and business succession goals, you are encouraged to seek the advice of your financial planner. Taking the time to observe your insurance coverages from many angles before you commit to ongoing premiums may help you avoid costly mistakes.

LIFE INSURANCE

There are two main classifications of life insurance: Temporary and Permanent.

Temporary insurance is known as Term Insurance, and it provides coverage for a set number of years. When the term is over, the insurance coverage ceases. The maximum number of years you may own a term policy is 30 years. Term insurance is the least expensive type available, so it is a great option for young families.

Permanent insurance is life insurance coverage that stays in existence for the lifetime of the insured as long as the premium is paid according to the terms of the insurance contract.

Whole Life Insurance is a permanent classification of life insurance. Part of the premium funds are used to pay for the cost of insurance, while another portion is used to create a Cash Value Account. The cash value account may be used to fund the increasing cost of insurance in your later years or may be available to you to use during your lifetime. Your cash value is accessible via a loan from your life insurance company, so note that you will pay interest on amounts used during your lifetime. Understand the terms before you sign.

Universal Life Insurance gives policyowners the ability to adjust their death benefit, premiums, and cash value. This gives great flexibility for a policyowner to pay more on the premium in a high-income year and less on the premium in a low-income year. This option reduces the risk of a policy lapse and is a great option for those with a need for permanent insurance.

A Variable Insurance Policy provides similar flexibility to adjust premiums, cash value, and death benefits. The added feature is the ability to personally direct and manage the cash value account by investing in securities. The cash value is divided into separate subaccounts and invested in stocks, bonds, and mutual funds chosen by the policyholder and a securities-licensed financial adviser. A higher risk tolerance is necessary because the investment risk is carried by the owner and losses may impact the sustainability of the policy. This type of insurance is a good fit for business succession, family legacy, and asset replacement planning.

Accelerated Death Benefit features provide funds to terminally or chronically ill insured persons while they are still living. For most life policies with this rider, up to 50% of death benefit values will be made available for qualified medical conditions.

A rider is an added benefit provision that is added to a life insurance contract. Qualified medical conditions may include dementia, Alzheimer's disease, loss of limb, stroke, heart failure, and loss of eyesight. Each accelerated death benefit or living needs feature has its own provisions, so read carefully for the coverages your contract provides.

To best determine whether temporary or permanent life insurance is most appropriate for you, explore the following considerations:

How much insurance do you need? What will the proceeds be used for?

How many years will you need coverage?

Does your risk tolerance allow you to comfortably invest in variable life insurance?

How much disposable income do you consistently have available?

Are you financially disciplined enough to sustain life insurance coverage?

What is your attitude toward leaving an inheritance to your heirs?

Long-Term Care Insurance

A standalone long-term care policy provides coverage for the costs of a skilled nursing facility. A comprehensive policy may also provide for in-home care and respite. Premiums for long-term care policies can be relatively expensive, and the premium is not guaranteed for the life of the policy. A common occurrence for this type of policy is a lapse in later years, before benefits can be used, due to the increases in premium costs. This type of policy requires a sustainable and increasing cashflow to provide confidence that it will not become cost-prohibitive.

Other than your age and health history, the cost of a premium will be determined by three factors: how long you wait, how much you get, and how long it lasts.

The first factor is how long you wait before the insurance coverage will begin once you have a qualified need for a claim. It is usually 90 days before your funds are available; however, some policies offer a shorter or longer elimination period.

The second factor is the amount of funds you will receive each day during a qualified skilled nursing facility stay. This could range anywhere from under $100 per day to over $300 per day.

The third factor effects the greatest variable on insurance premium costs. This factor addresses the length of months or years that the coverage is available and for which claim funds will be paid.

Adjusting any of these three elements of the long-term care policy will drastically change the premium, so if you are shopping rates, please be aware of the distinctions.

Your long-term care coverage claim will be payable upon a determination of a dementia disorder or the meeting of several ADL (activities of daily living) requirements. Most policies provide that if you are unable to do three or four of the following without assistance, you are qualified for coverage: feeding, transferring, toileting, bathing, dressing, and continence.

Be aware that some long-term care policies include provisions that make it impossible to meet one or more of the ADL requirements. For example, "If one cannot feed one's self through the use of utensil, plate, hands, or feeding tube, they will qualify as unable to feed without assistance." You have to wonder how this requirement could ever be met. Carefully study the long-term care policy provisions, which describe the details. Note that sales materials rarely provide the details of the contract provisions, so most people have no idea that their coverage may be compromised.

One alternative to the risks and costs of long-term care insurance is a Living Needs Rider contained in your life insurance policy. For little or no added premium, many insurance companies will add provisions to make funds available during your lifetime to cover your long-term care facility needs, serious medical conditions, or chronic illnesses.

This is a cost-effective way to provide coverage for you and your family in the likely event that someone in your family will need it at some point in the future. To be insurable, you must apply for a long-term policy while you are healthy, so if you believe you may want to be covered in the future, don't delay. You will want to plan while you can.

Don't Be Bullied by Sales People

Gretta and Dan Schwartz are empty-nesters. Both of their children have completed college. One is married, and Gretta and Dan are hoping to enjoy grandparenthood within the next few years. They are grateful that both children are living and working within an hour of their home in Indianapolis.

A few years back, Dan and Gretta attended a free dinner seminar that advertised complimentary information and consultations following the program. They enjoyed learning about the taxes and investment options in retirement and decided to schedule an appointment to meet with an "adviser."

In the meeting, they were instructed that the best way to achieve a successful retirement would be to "invest" $15,000 a year into a life insurance policy and reposition their retirement program contributions at work into an annuity their adviser highly recommended.

Not knowing any better, the Schwartzes followed instructions, signed the paper, and gave their sales representative access to all of their accounts. Within a year, the income taxes they owed increased by 40%, their cashflows became insufficient to sustain their monthly personal expenses, their personal consumer debt had increased by $18,000, and those repositioned investments were costing them $5,500 a year in fees.

They were in bad shape, and they weren't sure why.

When they approached their sales representative ("the nice man from the seminar"), he told them to "stay the course," and, "It's the best plan available," and, "Don't change anything." The only positive outcome from this whole series of transactions seems to have been in the interest of the sales representative. The commissions he earned on the transactions he recommended to the Schwartzes totaled over $43,000. Fortunately for the greedy sales representative, the Schwartzes did not dismantle the transactions until after his payday had been achieved.

In general, an online resource or insurance professional will be compensated by commission. The higher your premium, the more the commission or sales charges will be. Keep this in mind as you explore your investment and financial planning options.

To access more options to obtain cost-effective and appropriate insurance, or to learn whether your insurance policies are optimized, visit www.Judy Copenbarger.com/truth.

CHAPTER 8

HOW TO LIVE A LIFE OF INTEGRITY

If you were to examine the wheel of any bicycle, you would notice a pattern of features.

You'd find a circular tire on the rim at the perimeter, which is where the rubber meets the road. Then you would notice spokes all around the wheel. Each individual spoke connects to the center hub.

You could imagine that if any spoke of the wheel were to bend or become broken, the weakened spoke would impact each of the others. As additional spokes begin to bend or break, each causes an impact for others, enough so that eventually the integrity of the wheel becomes compromised. A total breakdown of the wheel may be inevitable.

It is at this point that, at best, the journey becomes difficult, and at worst, the journey becomes impossible.

Every spoke impacts every other spoke.

Everything affects everything.

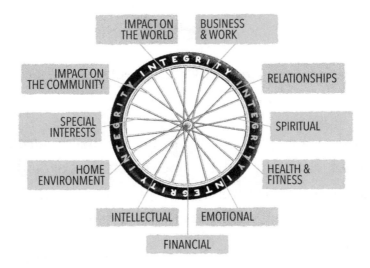

Now imagine that each spoke of this "integrity wheel" represents an area of your life. You have your business and work life; your relationships; your spiritual, emotional, and intellectual life; your health and fitness; your home environment; your special skills and interests; your impact on the community; and your impact on the world.

If an area of your life loses its integrity and that spoke becomes bent or broken, it is just a matter of time before other areas of your life will be negatively impacted.

Sometimes we see this when an individual loses their job. For no reason of their own, a move or a change in the economy or sector in which they work, they become unemployed. If they are out of work for a period, their emotional state may suffer, their financial life is impacted, and eventually their relationships suffer.

When someone is dealing with a health issue that lingers for a period of time, they may see a negative change in their relationships, as well as impact on their community and finances.

Everything affects everything.

Regarding home environment, when a lack of organization or cleanliness rises to the critical level of clinical hoarding, every other aspect of life begins to break down. The person ceases to have impact on the community, there is no engagement with neighbors, family relationships are severed, and finances are depleted. The emotional, spiritual, and physical wellness of people with an extremely poor home environment are compromised.

As you are reflecting on the various aspects of your life, take a moment to consider the state of something as simple as your home and living environment. How does your closet look? How about your garage? Would someone trust or hire you if they saw the condition of your storage space or the trunk of your car?

Yes, everything affects ... everything.

So if it is true that an area of life that lacks integrity will cause a loss of integrity in other areas of life, like the wheel spoke affecting each of the other spokes, then what are we to do?

Here's the good news. Like the bending or breaking spoke will affect all others, so does the straightening of a spoke. We can add integrity to one area of our life and experience the benefits in another. This is how life works.

For example:

You clean out your garage, and suddenly a profitable business idea occurs to you.

You implement a healthy eating and exercising program and subsequently find a way to profoundly impact your community.

You revisit hobbies you enjoyed as a child or before your career or parenting activities filled your calendar. Suddenly, your creative side awakens, and an unexpected and unprecedented source of income shows up for you.

You practice a spiritual habit, and the career of your dreams suddenly appears.

You insert a policy of excellence into your work, and suddenly optimal relationships seem to magically appear.

You pick up the phone to call that estranged friend or relative that you should have spoken to many years ago to clear up the misunderstanding. Even if you were the one who was right, imagine what could show up for you if you put integrity into your relationships.

What could show up for you?

- Money?

- Purpose?

- Relationships?

- Joy?

- Health?

- Peace?

Let's consider what spokes of our lives have lost their integrity. Which ones could we "straighten" to restore integrity and positively influence the important areas of our life?

CHAPTER 9

PREPARING YOUR NEXT STEPS

CREATING BALANCE

You may have read this book to learn how you can grow your wealth, gain knowledge about financial matters, or avoid money mistakes. You should be confident that you now know what most people don't. You have a collection of "money truths" that will help you better navigate your financial journey.

You'll have a broader perspective when you make financial decisions, and you'll be more equipped and empowered to make smart choices about money in your home and business. You are on your way to money mastery.

THE ELEMENTS OF MASTERY

In order to master anything, you need three elements. If any of the elements is missing, you can still achieve a moderate level of success, but that's it. Don't settle! In order to reach your potential and attain goals beyond your expectations, you will need mastery. Here are the three necessary elements for mastery: Knowledge, Resources, and Motivation.

1: Knowledge

This is your "know-how."

You will need to have an understanding of basic information. For a concert pianist to master his craft, he needs to know something about music.

As a small child, Theodore spent hours each day swinging his legs below the piano bench as he sat and picked away at the black-and-white keys. He learned music theory, how to count out the timing, how to harmonize the notes, and precisely how to use his foot pedals, arms, and fingers to bring the music on each page to life.

In college, he learned even more about piano technique, music genres, and the business of being a touring world-class pianist.

He could not have enjoyed success without the know-how of music, piano technique, business, and the art of performing.

He had attained element #1, Knowledge.

2: Resources

This is your "need it."

You will need resources in order to master whatever you put your mind to.

You would need resources to master a business. Perhaps you would need funding, equipment, good ideas, or personnel.

You would need resources for a world-class mountain climb. Perhaps you would need a support team, transportation, appropriate climbing gear and attire, and optimal hydration and nutrition elements.

At some point, Theodore, our world-class concert pianist, would have to have access to music, talented musicians to support his performances, and a stage. Imagine if he showed up onstage to play and had to stop to plug in his keyboard first. A grand piano is a necessary resource for his success.

3: Motivation

This is your "want to."

It doesn't matter how much you know and how equipped you are; you won't take action if you are not inspired. The third necessary element to mastery requires that you actually want to put in the effort to succeed.

Without motivation from the heart, it will be impossible to attain and sustain a successful mastery. So are you willing to actually do what it takes to get to the finish line?

To become profitable in your business, are you ready to withstand the expenses, setbacks, time constraints, fear, and negativity from your competitors? Do you have the motivation to break through when you want to break down?

To climb that mountain, are you willing to train your body, calendar the time for travel, and incur the expenses necessary to complete your journey to the summit? When it seems hopeless, do you have the motivation to remain hopeful and push on?

There were many times while sitting on that piano bench that Theodore wanted to walk away from those keys and never return. When he could hear the other children playing ball outside through the window near the piano where he practiced, his motivation to be the greatest pianist onstage kept him at the piano.

When Theodore considered the extreme expense of his advanced musical degrees, his desire kept him committed. At times, he thought he would never attain the bookings or be invited to perform in specific venues, but his desire and commitment to his dream gave him the motivation to stay on track, until he was performing on the largest world stages with the most talented musicians.

You will also master whatever you choose by gaining knowledge, obtaining resources, and sustaining motivation.

STRAIGHTENING YOUR "LIFE SPOKES"

As you are considering which of your Integrity Wheel spokes to straighten first, look to the area of life that will give you the most space. Having worked with thousands of individuals, families, and businesses over the past several decades, I have seen behavior patterns begin to emerge.

FINANCES AND FAITH

It has become apparent to me that Finances and Faith are two of the easiest spokes of life to "straighten."

In other words, it takes the least amount of your effort to gain the greatest results. So if you get excited about getting the most ROI (return on investment), this is life advice you may want to consider.

Finances and faith are the two areas of life you can improve in a great way with the least amount of effort. The reason is that these two areas of life are totally within your control. Your faith and finance choices don't require other people, time, or outside resources. There are no factors outside of your control that could undermine your progress. It is all you. Just choose to be on a new path, and you're there.

To improve your faith life, just choose God. It is so simple. Wherever you find your divine inspiration, go there.

You may be inspired by a church service or a visit to a temple or synagogue. Perhaps listening to some spiritual music, praise and worship, hymns, or the sounds of nature will bring you peace and a sense of freedom. Personally, I find a great sense of spiritual harmony and grounding in knowing that I was created by God to lead, educate, and inspire others.

When I am doing those things, I feel close to Him. I trust that He knows me better than anyone and has plans for my life to be my ideal life.

Whether it is your first time, a reboot, or you want to take your life to the next level, pick up a Bible and read it. Not only will this activity help improve your faith, but it is a fantastic source for financial advice. There are more references to money in the Bible than any other subject. Great resource!

In order to upgrade your financial life, take action. Stop doing those activities that are not serving you well. (You know what they are.) Check out our free YouTube videos (JudyCopenbarger) for tips and specific financial strategies. Be prepared to take notes.

You could gather our worksheets and templates, which will help you get your financial house in perfect order. Learn about our complete online money management course and how it can benefit your entire family through The **MONEY TRUTH & LIFE** *Online* **MASTERY PROGRAM**. You can read about it at the end of this book, or you can visit www.JudyCopenbarger.com/truth to get started.

By working toward improving the financial and faith areas of your life, you will discover improvements in other areas of your life as well. The most measurable result I regularly observe while working with financial clients is their increased peace around money. The level of marital harmony and family harmony raises to a high level, and although it doesn't appear that there would be a direct connection, I have learned that it is an undeniable outcome.

CREATING YOUR PLAN

Take some time to create your plan. How many days are there left in this year? Imagine what you could you accomplish by the end of the year if you start right now. So what do you need to do next?

1. Make a list of the five most important activities you will begin in order to move toward your ideal life.

2. Which activity is the most critical for you to succeed?

3. What can you do before you sleep tonight to make progress toward your #1 activity?

4. What would keep you from completing this activity?

5. Are you willing to overcome the barrier that threatens your success? What would it take for you to just CHOOSE to make progress toward your goal?

6. Now, channel your inner Nike, and ... "just do it!"

Appendix

Spending Plan Template for Families

Gross Income	$ 40,000	$ 60,000	$ 80,000	$100,000	$120,000
1. *Taxes (Estimated)	17.60%	21.10%	22.80%	19.70%	21.10%
2. Giving and Tithes	10%	10%	10%	10%	10%
Spendable Income	$ 28,960	$ 41,340	$ 53,760	$ 70,300	$ 82,680
3. Housing	55%	50%	45%	42%	40%
4. Utilities/Phone	2%	2%	2%	2%	2%
5. Food	10%	10%	10%	9%	9%
6. Transportation	10%	11%	12%	12%	12%
7. Insurance	4%	4%	4%	4%	4%
8. Tuition/Childcare (if applicable)	5%	5%	5%	5%	5%
9. Debt Repayment	4%	4%	4%	4%	4%
10. Savings (Cash Reserves)	1%	2%	3%	4%	5%
11. Investments (Future Goals)	1%	1%	3%	5%	5%
12. Wellness (Medical/Dental)	4%	4%	4%	4%	4%
13. Entertainment	1%	3%	3%	4%	4%
14. Clothing	1%	2%	3%	3%	4%
15. Miscellaneous (Holidays/Gifts)	2%	2%	2%	2%	2%
Total	100%	100%	100%	100%	100%

NOTES:

After contributing Taxes and Giving, Net Spendable Income is allocated for expenses and future goals.

Adjust your Spendable Income expenses, so the total always adds up to 100%.

Omit any expenses that do not apply, and reallocate the percentage from that expense category.

Remember this: Increasing the percentage of one category requires a reduction in another category.

*Tax estimates are based on a national average of combined federal and state taxes. (Married tax rates).

Seek the counsel of a qualified Financial Planner for your specific tax and expense situation.

LADDERING

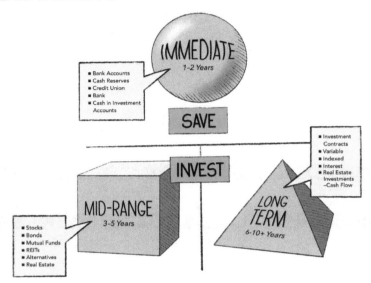

LADDERING

Laddering Instructions:

For NOW: Immediate Allocation:

How much money do you need in cash reserves?

How much money do you need for goals within 2 years?

Maintain this total amount in your savings.

For SOON: Mid-Range Allocation:

How much money will you need for your goals in 3–5 years?

Invest this amount for liquidity in balanced growth accounts.

For LATER: Long Term Allocation:

How much money will you need for expenses in 6 or more years?

How much money will you need to sustain you in your later years?

Protect this amount for safety in guaranteed growth accounts.

"Earn, Save, Sell" Exercise

For when the ends don't meet … . To improve your financial position, what are 10 things you can do in the next 30 days to <u>earn</u> more money, <u>save</u> more money, and <u>sell</u> something for money?

What could you create to sell, or what service could you provide? (Earn)

How could you decrease your spending and create new habits? (Save)

What possessions of value do you or your family no longer have use for? (Sell)

<u>Earn</u>, Save, Sell

What 10 things can you do to earn more money?

1.   6.

2.   7.

3.   8.

4.   9.

5.   10.

Earn, <u>Save</u>, Sell

What 10 things can you do to save more money?

1.   6.

2.   7.

3.   8.

4.   9.

5.   10.

Earn, Save, <u>Sell</u>

What 10 things can you sell to declutter and make your life simpler?

1.   6.

2.   7.

3.   8.

4.   9.

5.   10.

PAY OF CREDIT CARDS – 3 METHODS

(Choose One)

1. Ratio Method:

Add up your total debt and calculate the percentage of each credit debt, then apply new cash to the credit card bill using the same ratio.

Example:

$100 monthly available for credit card payments

AMEX	$600	= 60%	= $60 paid monthly
M/C	$300	= 30%	= $30 paid monthly
VISA	$100	= 10%	= $10 paid monthly

Note: You must make at least the minimum payment on each credit card account each month.

2. Interest Rate Method:

Pay off your highest interest rate cards first.

Example:

$165 monthly available for credit card payments

When the first account is paid off, payment amount is added to minimum payment amount of second account.

Amazon minimum	$15	(21% interest)
Macy's minimum	$35	(20.5% interest)
Home Depot minimum	$80	(18% interest)

Example:

Amazon (21% interest) make monthly payments of $50, rather than $15.

Once Amazon is paid off, the additional $50 will be added to Macy's (20.5% interest) minimum payments of $35, for a total of $85 paid monthly.

Once Macy's is paid off, the additional $85 will be added to Home Depot (18% interest) minimum payments of $80, for a total of $165 paid monthly.

Remember to continue making minimum payments on all other accounts while focusing on the account with the highest interest rate.

3. Balance Method:

Pay off your small balances first.

Each time an account is paid off, add the monthly payment amount to the monthly payment of next account to be paid off. (Next highest balance) Remember to continue making minimum payments on all other credit card accounts while focusing on the account with the smallest balance.

ABOUT THE AUTHOR

Your author is the profoundly caring, professional money guide **Judy L. Copenbarger, JD, CFP®, AIF®**. Judy counsels and patiently teaches individuals of all ages and families of all types on the real facts and agendas of money. She has put it *all* in writing for you in this eye-opening book to finally bring MONEY TRUTH to your life and into the lives of your entire family, *forever.*

An accomplished author and a sought-after speaker, Judy Copenbarger has penned several books while serving as a wise thought leader and an Accredited Investment Fiduciary, savvy about all family business and money matters. And she's your guide now!

Judy Copenbarger, as the Founder of MONEY TRUTH & LIFE, authored this book to share her expertise in Planning Personal & Family Finances. She makes sure you benefit from her deep experience *educating and protecting families* in intentional financial plans and estate planning strategies. She has served as the guide to families' futures for decades, <u>enabling families to live their ideal life</u> by putting in good order all things financial and legal.

Ms. Copenbarger is also the visionary Founder of *The Complete* MONEY TRUTH & LIFE *Online Mastery Program*, an online teaching and coaching system, which that provides solid and comprehensive training in money behaviors, financial planning, and family harmony around money *<u>to people from all walks of life</u>*. This life-changing *online* program also teaches people how to make all the money decisions that life requires and to make those decisions *in their best interest*.

A masterful teacher and easy to listen to, Judy uses colorful analogies and real-life lessons derived from her lifelong love of gardening, growing fruit tree orchards, and even raising rare breeds of chickens, which lay many colors of eggs.

Her practical wisdom and family harmony methods draw from raising her own five children to be financially sound and self-supporting. When their children were young, Judy and her husband, Larry, toured with them throughout the world, playing at musical venues from Carnegie Hall to Europe and the Sydney Opera House. Today they still enjoy family travel adventures and involvement in global ministries.

Ms. Copenbarger serves as president of Copenbarger Corporation, based in Newport Beach, California, and serves on boards and in volunteer roles for various philanthropic organizations.

Continue Online

HOW CAN YOU CONTINUE GROWING MONEY TRUTH IN YOUR LIFE?

CLICK and Launch Your Growth *Online*

- Simply plug into the *Online* Mastery Program available 24/7
- View videos in which Judy herself teaches and guides you
- Go beyond what you've begun learning in this book
- Share with others you love, your children and their children
- Watch videos as a family, learn & discuss together
- Receive the "tools" Judy has prepared to make you more successful
- Connect you and your family to practical wisdom that best serves your LIFE
- Know you have a high-integrity, life-changing program designed to serve YOU in your and your family's best interests.

Simply go to **www.JudyCopenbarger.com/Truth**
Don't lose any time now that you've begun your
MONEY TRUTH & LIFE journey.

GROUP DISCOUNTS:
CHARTER MEMBER, or GROUPS of 10 or more to purchase
additional copies of this book and the *Online* Mastery
Program at a special discount,
Contact us at: Copenbarger@gmail.com

CPSIA information can be obtained
at www.ICGtesting.com
Printed in the USA
LVHW080828250720
661486LV00012B/1648